NATURAL-BORN
INTUITION

How to Awaken and Develop Your Inner Wisdom

Lauren Thibodeau, Ph.D.

 New Page Books
A division of The Career Press, Inc.

NATURAL-BORN INTUITION
EDITED AND TYPESET BY KATE HENCHES
SOME INTERIOR ILLUSTRATIONS BY KATE PADDOCK
Cover illustration and design by Jean William Naumann

To order this title, please call toll-free 1-800-CAREER-1 (NJ and Canada: 201-848-0310) to order using VISA or MasterCard, or for further information on books from Career Press.

The Career Press, Inc., 3 Tice Road, PO Box 687,
Franklin Lakes, NJ 07417
www.careerpress.com
www.newpagebooks.com

Disclaimer: Anecdotes in this book are based on actual events, but identifying details have been changed to protect privacy.

Library of Congress Cataloging-in-Publication Data

Thibodeau, Lauren.
    Natural-born intuition : how to awaken and develop your inner wisdom /
by Lauren Thibodeau.
       p. cm.
    Includes bibliographical references and index.
    ISBN 1-56414-763-0 (pbk.)
       1. Intuition. 2. Self-actualization (Psychology) I. Title.

BF315.5.T44 2005
153.4'4--dc22

2004055998

DEDICATION

This book is dedicated to the thousands of people who have trusted me to help them know their way in the world, and to the many thousands more in the unseen world who share that world with me.

I am honored.

ACKNOWLEDGMENTS

The courageous pioneers in the fields of intuition, mediumship, and transpersonal psychology deserve note for their willingness to give voice to what they Know to be true. May the growing body of evidence that consciousness lives as much outside us as within us hearten the many researchers and practitioners who risked personal and professional attack for espousing controversial views. Thank you for opening the way.

To those who kept the flame burning when I could only see embers I owe a great debt of gratitude. Among the many colleagues and friends who deserve note are my muse Robin Blakely, my agent Joëlle Delbourgo, the professionals at New Page Books, and especially my psychotherapist husband Ed, who showed enormous patience and, more importantly, made me laugh.

Thank you all.

CONTENTS

FOREWORD

The process of coming to understand fully and completely who you are and why you are here is an ongoing journey of unfoldment and discovery. Through working with many thousands of clients and students through the years, I have borne witness to this journey and often served as a companion along the way. I'm grateful to all those clients and students whom I consider my teachers, for I've learned from each and every one.

In many ways, this is the story of my own journey as I try to piece together what it is that moves instinct to the level of intuition, and intuition to the level of a trusted sense of deeply guided Knowing. I've come to see instinct as the root, intuition the stem, and Knowing the beautiful blooming flower. So in some ways, this book, *Natural-Born Intuition: How to Awaken and Develop Your Inner Wisdom* is rather like a how-to guide for a beginning gardener. And just as no gardener is ever finished, none of us ever completes the inward journey toward self understanding.

Even so, this book is designed to make the inward journey less daunting by helping you understand yourself better. Through a series of self-tests (appraisals, really, because you can't fail), you'll determine your natural-born intuitive style. You'll learn your natural intuitive strengths and weaknesses. You'll learn your key values and how they interact with your natural intuitive style. You'll learn how those two elements—your natural intuitive style and your deeply held values—can launch you into that center of deeply guided inner wisdom, what I call the Knowing Zone. From there, you'll learn how to use a simple process called the *Four Corners of Knowing* to assess any decision both intuitively and analytically. That process ensures that you use *both* your creative right-brain hemisphere and your logical left-brain hemisphere.

The roots of this book extend far back in my own life. Blending the world of thinking with the world of feeling, the world of logical analysis with the world of creative expression, and the earthly world with the unseen world has been an ongoing journey since my childhood. Back then, I was known for what most people (including my kindergarten teacher) considered an overactive imagination and what my mother termed "brown outs." Those were times when I delivered accurate information that I couldn't have known through logical means. She called these psychic moments "brown outs" because, she logically noted, I wasn't completely blacked out. I now understand that I was tapping into unseen or spirit world quite naturally. This natural-born intuition caused many challenges, as well as much emotional pain throughout my school years, which is probably why I chose to study very logical subjects in college, notably engineering and economics.

Through this book, I hope to help you develop a fear-free, working understanding of your own natural intuition. With focus and conscious awareness, this understanding can lead you to an ongoing experience of deeply guided Knowing that gently directs you to the life you were meant to live and that encourages you to blossom into the fullness of all of who you are, into a Knowing Being.

INTRODUCTION

"From science and from the spiritual experience of millions, we are discovering our capacity for endless awakenings in a universe of endless surprises."

—Marilyn Ferguson

Learning to access—and more importantly, to follow—your inner wisdom, your soul's promptings, will lead you to a satisfying, balanced life of purpose and prosperity: the life you were born to live. Based on your natural-born intuitive style, your personal values, and the application of a simple four-step approach to decision making, the Knowing process I've created can lead you to experience a richer life. And, yes, that can include material wealth.

Through awakening and developing your Knowing, you'll gain control of your life. More importantly, you'll gain the power to transform it.

Living from Knowing brings you awareness of what your body and your health are asking of you. Living from Knowing helps you understand your life purpose, your unique calling. Living from Knowing helps you understand what steps you can take to improve relationships with family members, friends, and colleagues. Living from Knowing also helps you determine if taking those steps is worth the tradeoffs.

The cost of certain choices may include putting yourself out of balance or losing focus. Each and every one of your life choices has a benefit, a consequence, and a tradeoff. It can seem overwhelming. Many people simply freeze in place, afraid to make a decision at all.

Wouldn't it be helpful to feel more certain about the choices you make, to feel a deep resonance inside that tells you, "Yes, this is the right choice for me to make now"? You can awaken and develop a strong connection to that inner advisor, that powerful presence which I call your Knowing Self. In fact, you already have a strong connection to that wise Knowing Self, but, as most of us do, you probably lack clarity, consistency, and reliability when it comes to your own Knowing.

Isn't it time that changed?

I wrote this book to help you manifest that change. To help you learn to live from your Knowing Zone, that place deep within where your inner wisdom guides you wisely and well.

The first section of this book walks you step by step through five different areas of your natural-born intuition. You'll determine through a series of short self-appraisals what your natural intuitive strengths are. Whether you're Visual, Auditory, Sensory, Gut/Body-Based, or Mixed in your natural-born intuition, you'll discover ways to enhance, extend, and improve all five aspects of your intuition. Examples, anecdotes, development exercises called Inward Journeys, and immediate feedback tools called Power Points offer you a range of paths to develop your Knowing, allowing you to map your own road to inner wisdom.

The second section of this book helps you understand your personal values, using the chakra or energy center model, which uses the colors of the rainbow to differentiate levels of consciousness. Using simple self-assessment tools to help you better understand your values, you'll determine where your deeply held values match up against your natural-born intuitive style. The result is a Knowing Self-Portrait, which shows how your intuitive strengths and your values interact to provide highly reliable areas of Knowing. With this awareness you'll make better informed choices. Choices that resonate, that "fit" your life, and that allow your Knowing Self to shine.

The last section of this book introduces you to a process that I call the Four Corners of Knowing. By assessing major life decisions from each of four places—Intention, Attention, Reflection, and Evolution—you'll find you can consistently make choices that feel completely right and move you toward your self-fulfillment. Even if things don't turn out as expected (and that's always a possibility, given that every one of the seven billion of us here has free will to choose and thus to mess up your best-laid plans), you'll always Know you made your decision from a place of fully engaged conscious awareness.

The Appendices offer you additional tools and resources, including examples of how to keep a Knowing Journal to document your progress, suggested reading, informative Websites and reflections, and exercises to play with as you seek to open to your inner wisdom.

What to Expect

As you work with the material in this book, particularly if you're consistent about it, you'll unleash a powerful sense of ongoing, fully engaged conscious awareness: Knowing. As you approach each life decision, you'll be able to discern what you'll gain and what it will cost you. You'll be better prepared to decide what choices to make, and when to make them. You'll make those choices with flexibility, grace, and wisdom. You'll make them calmly and without regrets. By learning how to live from your Knowing Zone, you will be able to:

* Garner creative insights in any problem-solving situation—even scientific or technical ones—through your personal Knowing shorthand symbolism.

* Understand and use the insights your dreams offer you—and *only* you.

* Improve relationships with family members, friends, colleagues, and lovers through deepened empathy.

* Find, or create the perfect career—and then continue to make the best strategic moves to further enhance your success.

* Present your views calmly and with conviction, confidence, and clarity—and without worrying what other people will think.

* Meet your ideal life partner—and truly Know if he or she is best for you.

* Learn to preview possible outcomes of any decision you are considering. This allows you to make the best choices because you'll be ready for just about anything.

* Bask in the centered, balanced inner glow that discovering and purposely building a relationship with your own Knowing Self brings.

My goal in *Natural-Born Intuition* is to encourage you to actively use this book as a blueprint to your inner wisdom, your Knowing Self. During this process, you may discover it's time for some new additions or some serious renovations to your life. You may decide to let go of some long-held beliefs that no longer serve you. You may break through some blocks that have kept you from achieving your full potential. You may finally give yourself permission to hear the subtle call of your own Knowing, the voice of your own spirit, the song of your own soul. And you may feel as though certain aspects of your life are falling down around you as we progress.

That may be unsettling, but please, bear with the process. Renovations are messy. They take time. Dust flies everywhere. And they don't always turn out exactly the way you expected. But remember free will? It means that if you don't like the changes, you can redo and rebuild until you get it exactly as you like.

Rest assured that your inner architect, your inner wisdom, Knows the blueprints of this wonderful house. Your inner wisdom can handle any adjustments and updates. In fact, your Knowing Self will probably suggest some excellent ideas for you to consider.

I'd say, "Let's get started," but the inward journey to your own Knowing is already underway.

It always has been.

I'm grateful that you've decided to join me on this journey into your wise inner being, your Knowing Self.

I promise you one simple thing: more from your life.

CHAPTER 1
THE BASIS OF KNOWING

"Perhaps the greatest false truth is that some people are not intuitive, as if this key survival element was somehow left out of them."

—Gavin de Becker, *The Gift of Fear* (Little Brown & Co., 1997)

Right from the beginning, I want to assure you that you *are* intuitive. You have all the foundational elements and building blocks necessary to live from that place of inner wisdom, the place I call Knowing. You were born with a unique genetic blueprint, and within that blueprint is a particular and unique intuitive style. Just as people vary in eye color, skin tone, height, and weight, they vary in terms of their natural intuitive style. But it's *always* there. It may be hidden under the surface, but it's there. It's as much a part of you as the blood coursing through you right this minute. It's as much a part of you as your digestive system, which even now is working to keep you sustained, supported, and energized.

You generally don't think too much about your blood flow or your digestion (unless it's bothering you for some reason) and, yet, you rely on these unacknowledged systems, trusting that they're there when needed, efficiently doing their jobs in the background. Intuition is much the same way; it operates without much assistance from you. In fact, its purpose is to assist *you* rather than the other way around. Before we delve into the how-to's of Knowing, let's take a look at some background and establish some ground rules and terms that I'll be using throughout this book.

Your Intuition Is Always Right

Your natural-born intuition is always "right" in that it always wants to help you. In fact, the word *intuition* is based in the Latin term *tuere* which means "to guard or to protect." So if you think of your Knowing as a sort of personal guardian angel, particularly because it has the potential to move you quickly to a life-saving decision in times of danger, you won't be far off the mark.

Where we miss the full impact of intuition, where we get it wrong, is in the interpretation. Generally, I prefer to avoid using terms such as "right" and "wrong" because they are loaded with judgments. Of course, feedback matters and is a critical aspect of learning. But instead of focusing on your intuitive hits and misses—your "rights" and "wrongs"— as you work with this material, I encourage you to focus on the experience of being in the Knowing Zone, that place where you feel deeply connected and able to tune in to your deepest, wisest inner being.

The Ground Upon Which Knowing Stands: The Inward Journey

Natural-born intuition benefits from reflection and contemplation, which is why you'll find Inward Journey exercises throughout this book. The ability to tune in is developed through the Inward Journey of paying attention to your own way of Knowing, to seeking to understand your own intuitive strengths and weaknesses. It takes time, and attention, but I promise you, the Inward Journey toward Knowing will make the simple black-and-white distinctions of "right" and "wrong" far less important. That's because in the Knowing Zone, you experience a richer, textured, broader perspective communicated to you through your natural-born intuition, your own Knowing shorthand, your personal symbolism. Your personal values are a key aspect of those symbols and the meanings you associate with them.

Through these shorthand symbols, which require that you pay attention to your body and mind, you'll understand what each potential choice is likely to bring you in terms of rewards and tradeoffs. Being able to make more informed decisions is far more helpful to thriving in your life than simply focusing on "right" and "wrong" bits of data. So as you learn to trust your Knowing, you'll learn to pay attention to the process and the patterns as well as the hits and misses.

The Roots of Knowing

Knowing is rooted in your natural-born intuition, which is deeply biological. It's not a special gift, but a birthright once used for survival. Our ancestors relied on intuitive instinct to make snap decisions that often had life-or-death consequences. Those with a greater degree of natural-born intuition survived. Over subsequent generations, natural selection meant that each generation had stronger, more reliable natural-born or innate instincts than those of previous generations. This is a key reason why so many children these days evidence powerful intuition from very young ages.

As we became increasingly removed from the natural world, we had less need for life-or-death, fight-or-flight instinct. But the "hard wiring" of life-saving instinct, strengthened by natural selection, remained. Today, we call the remnants of that deeply rooted instinct intuition. And it still serves us.

Intuition is like gravity: it's just there. Gravity doesn't care whether you believe in it or not, or understand it or not. Neither does intuition. They both operate in our world, regardless of your belief system or level of understanding of the underlying principles. But the greater your understanding of gravity, the better you can use it to your advantage and save yourself considerable time and effort. The same applies to intuition.

Even if you consider yourself a skeptic (I believe a true skeptic is open to new ideas. Modern forms of skeptical inquiry recognize that concepts are not "…fixed or final and may be modified in the future by future observations and theories." [Paul Kurz in *Should Skeptical Inquiry Be Applied to Religion?*, *Skeptical Inquirer*, July/August 1999]), please try the techniques in this book. Like the guy who figures out that working *with* the force of gravity makes life easier, you may discover that working with your intuition, accessing your Knowing, also makes life easier. See for yourself what works and what doesn't. Keep a log of your progress, a personal Knowing Journal (see Appendix B for suggestions). Use it as a scientist would: to keep a record of your experiments on the road to new discoveries, to your own Knowing. Be patient with yourself. Thomas Edison experimented with thousands of approaches that didn't work before perfecting the ones that did.

Knowing vs. Knowledge, Process vs. Product

Throughout this book, Knowing is spelled with a capital K to differentiate it from knowledge. Knowing is a process. Knowing is Now. Knowing is internal, personal, subjective. It's *always* about you and it always operates in the present moment. Knowing is a *process*.

Knowledge is historical, is external, and operates in the past. Knowledge is a *product*, an outcome of inquiry, reflection, and analysis. Based on collected observations, often rooted in the structured methods of empiricism and science, knowledge is considered more objective than Knowing (although even Albert Einstein admitted his fondness for intuition as a useful tool in scientific discovery, claiming, "The really valuable thing is intuition."). Usually, knowledge is "common," meaning shared or experienced by many. As a result, knowledge is generally about the collective, and applicable to many. An example is the common knowledge of plant lore that guided our ancestors and still helps us today.

Alignment: Left Brain Meets Right Brain

Your Knowing works best when you align your right brain's inner wisdom with your left brain's rational knowledge. Just like a worker moves heavy loads more easily with knowledge and the assistance of gravity, your knowledge helps your Knowing, and vice versa. Objective knowledge feeds and sustains intuitive Knowing; Knowing in turn illuminates and elucidates knowledge. Think of the relationship between Knowing and knowledge as an infinity symbol. Together, the two loops feed, extend, and expand our potential for understanding to an infinite level where anything, and everything, is possible. The most powerful point in the diagram in Figure 1 is the place where the two loops of the infinity symbol meet, where logic meets sensation, where thought meets feeling.

Knowing Meets Knowledge:
The Infinite Connection

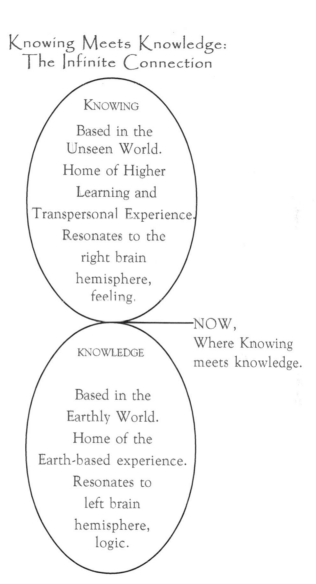

KNOWING

Based in the
Unseen World.
Home of Higher
Learning and
Transpersonal Experience.
Resonates to the
right brain
hemisphere,
feeling.

—NOW,
Where Knowing
meets knowledge.

KNOWLEDGE

Based in the
Earthly World.
Home of the
Earth-based experience.
Resonates to
left brain
hemisphere,
logic.

Figure 1

If you choose to access only one loop, approaching decisions and tasks entirely from logic, or entirely from feeling, you're limiting yourself. By using *both* your logic and your feeling centers, your left and right brain hemispheres, you expand your potential infinitely. The creative right brain, where Knowing lives, and the analytical left brain, where knowledge is at home, can be trained to work together. In fact, they're designed to work together, the way your right and left hands are. The power is in the partnership between Knowing and knowledge, in the link between right-brain insights and left-brain analyses, in the connection between insights in the present moment Now and the powerful historical data gleaned from passed "nows."

The whole *is* greater than the sum of its parts. As Albert Einstein said, "The intuitive mind is a sacred gift and the rational mind is a faithful servant. We have created a society that honors the servant and has forgotten the gift."

It's time to unwrap the gift of your Knowing. But because you've picked up this book, you probably Know that already.

What Knowing Correlates to

This place of Knowing has some affiliation to the superego (to use the terminology of Sigmund Freud), the collective unconscious (in Carl Jung's schema), the Godhead, Universe or Creator (in theological and metaphysical terms). It's also been called the supraconscious, the Godhead, the Universal mind, the Great Intelligence, the higher self, Enlightenment, the Absolute, the Atman, the One, the All that Is (and Is Not), the oversoul, God, and many other terms. Use whichever term you prefer or make up your own; for the purposes of this book, I shall call it the Unseen World to differentiate it from the Earthly World in which we live while in human form.

Your relationship to the Unseen World is uniquely *yours*; at the same time, the Unseen World is shared with everyone else. A good analogy is this Earth: your relationship to the planet is uniquely yours, and you haven't seen all of it, nor will you in your lifetime. Maybe you like forests, whereas your friends prefer deserts, mountains, islands, beaches, or caves. Just as we don't all have the same relationship with the Earthly World, we don't all have the same relationship with the

Unseen World, and we are not meant to. That's one reason that there are many paths of self-discovery to investigate. The gathered wisdom of many people over thousands of years, a nonreligious view called the Perennial Philosophy by Aldous Huxley in his book of the same name (Perennial Classics, 2004), points out the Inward Journey is one which leads to connection to something larger than ourselves, whatever you choose to call it. I call it Knowing.

Just as there are many unexplored corners of this Earth, so too are there many unexplored corners of the Unseen World. And just as you choose where you live or travel on this Earth, so too do you choose what and where you want to explore in the Unseen World. You won't see all of it, either. Don't let the achievement model of the Western world get in your way. The journey is the point, not the destination. In fact, there is no destination, because we are stuck here in the eternal moment, Now, and we *never* actually reach a destination. We reach a state of mind. Knowing is the personalized form of this higher state of mind, and it applies solely to you and your life.

That's why reaching for those realms of higher understanding, of inner wisdom, requires you to start with Knowing your Self. Bridging the Unseen World with the Earthly World through your own Knowing is the journey you are on, that we all are on. As Shakespeare put it so well, "To thine own self be true."

When Worlds Collide

As everyone else has, you've had moments when the two worlds "collided." Many moments, in fact. These have been called peak experiences, Spiritually Tranformative Experiences (STEs), and a variety of other terms. Recall a time when you felt so completely connected to nature that time seemed to stop, so loving toward someone that you felt as if you had merged into one being, so peaceful that you would have been happy to stay in that space for eternity, so awed by a religious experience or so moved by a near-death experience that you felt completely connected to something beyond yourself.

Understanding this process allows you to row with the tides, not against them, to move in the flow of the currents between the Unseen World and this Earthly World. If we get "stuck" in our lives, we continue to be faced with the same situation in different forms, over and over again until we learn to row with the tides. At those "stuck" points, we're vainly striving to stay in the same cycle, hoping to be like a swimmer who never changes lanes but keeps doing lap after lap.

Ever feel like you dated or married the same personality in a different body a few times, or witnessed a friend do so? Or kept finding the same types of unfulfilling work assignments, over and over? Those are definitely clues that it's time to change lanes. It's time for an Inward Journey.

This blending of logic and insight, of right-brain hemisphere and left-brain hemisphere through the Knowing process, is fed by the energies of Unseen World (the upper loop of the infinity symbol turned like an eight) and your experience in the Earthly World (the lower loop of that figure eight; see Figure 1 on page 17). Learning to actively engage the Unseen World with the Earthly World will guide you to a place of inner calm, of pure awareness, of inner wisdom. A placed called your own Knowing.

A comparison to a scientific principle will make this more clear. Remember that certain parts of the light spectrum, such as the infrared, aren't visible to the naked eye, although they exist. Their higher rates of vibration make them seem invisible, but they're real. Your Knowing Self is like a broad-spectrum light pattern, a fully accessible version of you; it's "bigger, better, more," if you will. This book is designed to teach you how to allow your bigger-better-more-Knowing Self to inform and guide your journey on Earth. At the same time, your Earthly presence and the choices you make here actually alter the Unseen World. The following diagram shows graphically the Earthly World/Unseen World relationship.

The Two Worlds: Infinite Interaction

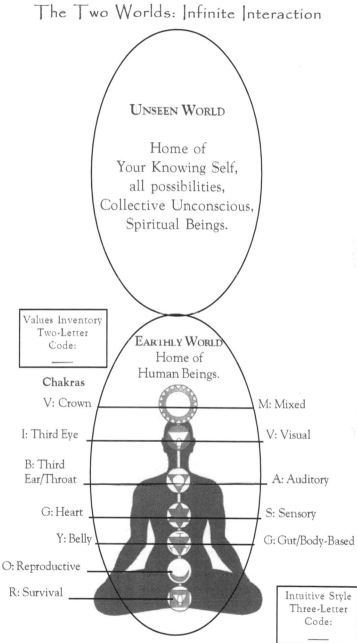

UNSEEN WORLD

Home of
Your Knowing Self,
all possibilities,
Collective Unconscious,
Spiritual Beings.

Values Inventory
Two-Letter
Code:
____

EARTHLY WORLD
Home of
Human Beings.

Chakras

V: Crown

I: Third Eye

B: Third
Ear/Throat

G: Heart

Y: Belly

O: Reproductive

R: Survival

M: Mixed

V: Visual

A: Auditory

S: Sensory

G: Gut/Body-Based

Intuitive Style
Three-Letter
Code:
____

Figure 2

Your Knowing Self-Portrait

An expansion of the image from the lower loop of the infinity symbol (shown in Figure 1 to represent the Earthly World) will help you create what I call your Knowing Self-Portrait. It's designed as a single place where you can record the self-assessment information you'll gather on your journey through this book. Feel free to make an enlarged copy of the blank Knowing Self-Portrait image found in Appendix A. You may want to keep a working copy in your Knowing Journal, too. Suggestions for journaling are found in Appendix B.

Knowing Is Always "Now"

Knowing is *always* present tense. That's because this present moment, the Now, is all we ever have in which to make choices. Certainly reviewing your history and focusing forward on your dreams and goals are important, but decisions always happen in the moment, Now. Living from Knowing is a way of being ever-present in the moment. It's also a way of deliberately interacting with a greater degree of your consciousness. It's living with your inner wisdom switched on, your consciousness more fully engaged. Living from your natural-born Knowing, that deeply guided, fully trusted sense of what's right for you, will take you places you never imagined were possible. And it will keep fear of change from running your life.

Releasing the Fear Factor

When you align the Earth World and the Unseen World, using both your Knowing and your knowledge, life is enhanced. Emotions are felt, but no longer rule you. Relationships flow more easily. Work—even work you don't like, or that is beneath your talents and training—becomes rewarding for its own sake, for the process itself. Life lived from Knowing continues in a perpetual, self-fulfilling cycle of movement, growth, and change, like an ever-expanding infinity symbol. Knowing is one loop, knowledge the other, and there's no room for fear.

This is because as you work on blending your Knowing and your knowledge, an even more powerful shift happens. Fear of change, which stops so many people from achieving their full potential, is released.

Why? Because you no longer need to fear change. It's just part of the process as the "loops" of Knowing and knowledge expand and evolve. When you have a deep connection to your own Knowing, fear no longer fits; you'll find you've outgrown it.

Actually, you'll have transformed it. As you build bridges between Knowing and knowledge, between your rational left brain and your intuitive Knowing, between the ever-present Now and the past, fear becomes fuel for change, rather than a block to progress. Fear will actually become a motivator, because your Knowing and your knowledge, your intuitive right brain and your analytical left brain, the gift of your intuition and the servant of your rational mind, will be working together. As your ancient ancestors did, you'll realize that fear is simply a sign to move. Through ongoing practice, you'll learn to Know in which *direction* to move. The old saying "knowledge is power" becomes a new reality, one where Knowing adds even *more* power, because your inner wisdom, your full potential, is awakened.

Bridging the Gap

Bringing knowledge and Knowing together requires a willingness to work systematically until your Knowing is internalized, the way a radar system that alerts you to what really matters. When you stop fighting your Knowing (or placing Knowing below knowledge rather than seeing it as an equal partner), you'll find your life works better—infinitely better.

But to build this bridge to Knowing, of course, takes—you guessed it—knowledge. Your analytical mind needs something to chew on. Just saying "trust your intuition" or "listen to that voice inside" isn't enough to keep your left brain well fed and well rested. Your left brain keeps coming back, keeps trying to objectively observe, to create knowledge from the process of Knowing. It's that same part of your mind that wanders off repeatedly when you're trying to meditate.

Your intuitive mind keeps nudging knowledge along, too. It wants to pull knowledge aside and whisper, "Hey, there's more to this, if you let yourself go a bit, into the flow, into the feeling." The Aha! moments of discovery that so many scientists have experienced are excellent examples of this phenomenon.

Andrew Wiles, who resolved the proof of mathematician Fermat's last theorem, said, "Suddenly, unexpectedly, I had this incredible revelation." Isaac Newton was taking a bath when he immediately, clearly understood displacement in his "Eureka!" moment. Certainly their left-brain hemispheres filled with scientific knowledge created fertile ground for the deeper Knowing of these ground-breaking scientists to take root when they switched on their Knowing right-brains (even if they did so accidentally). And as they did for Wiles and Newton, knowledge and Knowing working together can lead you to discoveries beyond your wildest imagination, to some very sweet fruits.

Just like the development of any skill or talent, awakening and developing your inner wisdom require focus and practice. But I promise you, if you work with the techniques you'll learn in this book (and maybe even create some of your own), you will find yourself deeply immersed in the journey toward your own inner wisdom. This journey of unfoldment, of learning to honor your own Knowing, helps you understand your way in the world, your place in the universe.

That's the journey I want to guide you along: the journey to your *own* Knowing, a journey that will simplify and immeasurably enrich your life, the journey toward feeling the wisdom of your Heart, hearing the voice of your Spirit, singing the song of your Soul.

Are you ready for the adventure?

CHAPTER 2
THE LIMITS OF KNOWING

"The richness of the human experience would lose something of rewarding joy if there were no limitations to overcome."

—Helen Keller

Knowing is not all-powerful and it's not infallible. There are limitations in this Earthly World, such as living in a human body. We can't fly no matter how strongly we intend that as a goal. Yet one of the blessings of life here is free will, which serves as a way we can test, expand, and often overcome some perceived limits as we learn and grow.

Learning to understand and appropriately apply your free will in all its dimensions is powerful stuff. Through accessing your Knowing Self, you'll make decisions informed by your intention to make the best possible free will choice under any circumstances. In doing so, you also will be uplifting the human energy field, actually improving the course of human development. Given that the misuse of free will is a root cause of all the difficulties mankind faces, that's a wonderful way to focus your energies: toward the higher vibration of the Unseen World represented by that upper loop of the infinity symbol (see Figure 2, on page 21).

The Efficiency Effect

For the purposes of this book, suffice it to say that your free will develops exponentially as you develop your inner Knowing wisdom. As that inner wisdom evolves, a smaller input from you in the form of a thought, whether positive or negative, other-directed or self-focused, creates a greater output. You become what I call energetically efficient, and that affects the Unseen World as well as this one.

When you join groups and work together, whether in person, online, or from a distance (such as in prayer and healing circles), the group's spiritual and energetic efficiency builds. Many studies show that the power of prayer can be documented, as Larry Dossey's work points out so well. Exactly how it works may not be completely discerned at this time (true also for aspirin) but *that* it works is quite well documented (just like aspirin!). So even if you're a skeptic (not a debunker, a skeptic systematically evaluates new input; debunkers refuse to), why not experiment? See what impact you can create through the development of energetic efficiency. Although it's true that negatively intended groups could also develop a level of energetic efficiency, the higher, finer "goodness" vibe that well-intended groups bring means they always outperform negatively focused groups. As the saying goes, good triumphs in the end.

Many resources on the development of inner life, personal power, and manifesting refer to this quality of energetic efficiency, although they use other terms for it. Energetic efficiency is developed through ongoing practice, living consciously in the moment Now, and evaluating the outcomes—expected, unexpected, positive, or negative—of the choices we make from our free will.

As you develop your Knowing, you'll be developing energetic efficiency, too, which may be the best gift of Knowing. That's because it brings an important practical aspect to the application of your intuition. We need practical approaches here in the Earthly World. By training yourself to use both your logic and your intuition, both your left brain and your right brain, and to quickly scan your various intuitive shorthand symbols, you'll be consciously choosing to be better informed, and that's a very wise free-will choice.

Compassion in Action

A brush with death, directly or indirectly, is often a doorway to inner wisdom. For this reason, one of the most powerful spiritually transformative experiences, also called STEs, is the near-death experience. Through what Daniel Goleman termed emotional intelligence in his groundbreaking book by the same name (Bantam, 1997), and what others call deep empathy or compassion, we can imagine the experiences of others. The better we become at doing that, the easier it is to Know our way in the world. Why? Because we've "practiced" by asking ourselves, "What would I do in that situation?" and letting our inner wisdom, our Knowing Self, answer.

The Unfoldment of Knowing

I created the Knowing approach over many years of observing clients, teaching students, and coaching practitioners in the development and unfoldment of their natural intuitive talents. Among the first things I realized is that the traditional way of classifying intuition is too limiting. The classical terminology fails to adequately express the unique intuitive talents expressed by each and every one of the more than seven billion people who currently share this Earthly World. Just as we each have a distinct voiceprint and fingerprint, we also have a distinct intuition-print, what I call an Intuitive Style.

You may already be familiar with the classic interpretation of the intuitive or psychic senses. *Clairvoyance* means clear seeing; clairaudience means clear hearing; clairsentience means clear sensing. A fourth term, used less often, is clairgustience, which means clear tasting. *Clairolfactory* sense means clear smelling and is rarely used. Recently, the terms *clairknowing* and *claircognition* have been used to represent the experience of an accurate, intuitive flash of insight, what I call a Knowing Moment.

One problem I've come across is that most people feel far from clear when their intuition flashes. Usually, they're either confused and want to shrug off the experience, or they turn immediately to a left-brain-based, logical interpretation to explain their Knowing Moments. A second, bigger problem I discovered is that the terms *clairvoyance, clairaudience, clairsentience, clairgustience,* and *clairolfactory* suggest that intuition is unusual, or that it operates on only one sensory channel at a time. Neither is true.

Intuition is often called a "gift" or a "sixth sense," which makes it seem like something outside ourselves, beyond our control, mysterious, and unpredictable. Well-trained intuition is none of those things. The program outlined in this book will teach you how to train your intuition, how to master the five basic "building blocks" of intuition: the Visual, Auditory, Gut/Body-Based, Sensory, and Mixed response styles.

Your Unique Intuitive Style

Intuition is not different from our five senses of vision, hearing, touch, taste, and smell, but rather an *extension* and *blend* of them, which also incorporates *each person's unique life experience and values*. This is a critical differentiating factor—and it's why so many people who've tried a one-size-fits-all approach to intuitive development often report being baffled, frustrated, and distrusting of their own Knowing. Your deeper mind—the messy basement where your life experiences are stored—is a big player in your own Knowing. Gaining access, clearing the clutter, and building a new foundation for your Knowing are important steps.

The five building blocks to your Knowing will be addressed in the Chapters 3 through 12. Just as a personal trainer at the gym helps you work your muscles from head to toe, you'll have a chance to work on all five building blocks for your inner wisdom. Some exercises will feel comfortable and natural for you, and some won't. Just as your body needs to have all its muscles stretched and exercised for its greatest health and wellness, so too does your Knowing need all its foundational muscles stretched and strengthened to be at the peak of reliable performance. As you work your way through the five core areas, you'll develop a two-letter code that serves as "shorthand" for your natural-born intuitive style.

To reach that trusted sense of reliable, moment-by-moment life guidance called Knowing, you'll also be encouraged through exercises I call Inward Journeys and quick feedback tools I term Power Points. Keeping a journal of your experiences, a book of the revisions to your mental mansion blueprints, is encouraged (suggestions for how you might do this are found in Appendix B). Thought-provoking questions designed to help you reclaim your passion and discover your life purpose—a key element of living in the Knowing Zone is fulfilling your chosen destiny—are in Appendix C. And yes, you must meditate or regularly take quiet time for the best results from your Knowing Self. But don't panic. Even if you think you can't meditate, I promise you, you can learn, and it doesn't have to be an elaborate process. You'll find tips for simplifying the meditation process and building it into your life in Appendix D.

While you're encouraged to work through the book one chapter at a time, if you'd rather ramble aimlessly wherever you feel drawn, that's fine, too. Just be sure that you take the six-question self-appraisal of each intuitive building blocks (found on pages 39, 60, 80, 98, and 115). The five building blocks, along with your experiences with Inward Journeys and Power Points, will provide you with valuable, personalized insights about the unique way *your* intuition, *your* inner wisdom, *your own* Knowing operates.

After working with the Knowing system consistently for a few weeks, you'll be well on your way toward building lifelong foundations of Knowing, which can guide you in how to best live your life for decades to come. Sounds like a long time? It won't feel that way, because through Knowing, you will find yourself ever present in the moment, living fully, Now.

What's It All Mean?

Before we get into your own natural-born intuitive style—we'll get there, I promise—I first want to clear up any confusion about terminology. You may have had some of the experiences that follow. While they all have an intuitive or Knowing quality, they aren't at the level of inner wisdom. Inner wisdom, that Knowing place, is deeper, richer, quieter, and much more consciously tuned and reliable.

The following are working, practical definitions and do not reflect all levels of possibility, but are meant to give you a basic understanding of what you may experience as you deepen your capacity for inner wisdom.

Instinct: The fight-or-flight survival response that is "hard-wired" as part of our human biology. Instinct is the lowest level of Knowing. It's primarily body-based and kicks in when survival is a concern. Instinct tells us to run, now. Instinct is present-moment awareness.

Intuition: Knowing without knowing how we know, inner aware-ness without logical thought while conscious. One level up from instinct, intuition is responsible for "flashes" of insight. Instinct tells us to run, but intuition guides us regarding *in which direction* to run. Intuition often has a precognitive quality, which allows the course of events to be changed. Precognitive intuition is most reliable when re-lated to personal situations, less reliable in predicting group events. Timing generally is not a reliable aspect of intuition, although it can be improved through practice and documentation to detect timing pat-terns. Intuition can be considered the point where the conscious mind meets the subconscious mind. It is associated with the creative side of our brain, the right hemisphere, usually abbreviated to "right brain." Intuition may draw on the past, present, or future for insight.

Psychic Ability: Psychic ability is picking up on the signals oth-ers are broadcasting. Psychic ability may be past-, present-, or future-oriented, but, in general, use is considered future-focused. The term *psychic* is often used to mean intuitive, although the two concepts are very different. Psychics reach out for information, while intuitives delve inward for Knowing. Intuition is a personal, inward journey that fo-cuses on *receiving*; psychic ability is an outbound journey that focuses on the *broadcaster*.

Psychic ability is necessary for working with other people as an intuitive consultant, but a wise intuitive always goes *inward* for infor-mation—it's far less stressful to the body, mind, and spirit. It's also less likely to draw frightening or negative experiences toward the practitio-ner. Most people reach the level of psychic ability first and intuitive ability later. Many people get "stuck" at the psychic level and never develop their full capacities for Knowing. While developing psychic ability is an important step on this path, working from Knowing is much more rewarding (and easier, when you get the hang of it).

Precognitive Dreams: Precognitive dreams are intuitive experi-ences that happen during the dream state and generally warn of physi-cal danger. They are rooted in the survival instinct of the dreamer, although they may involve others (which means they sometimes have a psychic, as well as intuitive, quality). Precognitive dreams sometimes bring forth information from the subconscious, which is then "worked" by the dreamer's intuition for a deeper level of understanding, which may come via additional dreams, or intuitive flashes ,which I call Knowing Moments. Training and focusing the mind through meditation reduces precognitive dreams and increases waking awareness, or Knowing. Precognitive dreams are future-oriented by nature, but may contain insights about the past and present.

Mediumship Ability: The ability to sense the unique energies of a person who has died and convey that information accurately, usually to someone who knew the individual and who can confirm the information. The most familiar form of mediumship and is called message mediumship in which, by nature, the message is focused on the past (or on details of a passed-on person's life). As is intuition, mediumship is an inward journey; from a centered, deeply internal place, a skilled medium is able to allow departed persons to communicate through thought. Nearly all mediumship practiced today, even trance mediumship or channeling, is essentially mental and based in thought, even when the body of the medium is used to convey information by gesture or speech. The brain receives thoughts and impressions which use the medium's neurological system to create gestures and speech. It all begins with thought and, thus, is mental.

As with Knowing, psychic skill is a prerequisite for quality mediumship. Over time, mediumship generally evolves beyond understanding the perspectives of departed humans and may become a general sense of guidance from a higher source such as angels, guides, or groups of spiritual teachers. In this way it moves toward Knowing.

Visitation Dreams: Visitation dreams actually are mediumship experiences that happen during the dream state. They generally involve memorable experiences of "meeting with" people who have died and are most common during the first few years after a death, and with those to whom we had strong emotional ties. Deep grief and longing may reduce and/or delay the probability of visitation dream. The reason is that strong emotions of any type, but especially anger, fear, guilt, and remorse create what I call "vibrational static," which reduces the capacity to receive visitation dreams. These dream experiences are almost always positive experiences and easily, vividly recalled even years or decades later.

You may have had other intuitive, psychic, or spiritual experiences that don't fit neatly into the previously mentioned categories. That's fine, and expected. Mystical experiences occur more frequently for many people as they learn about and train their intuition and extend it into Knowing. Others have experienced such blissful and personally sacred mystical moments that led them to approaches, such as this one, which will help them contain and control their intuitive flashes. Still others experience what psychologist Abraham Maslow called peak experiences—moments of connection to something far larger than oneself such as near-death experiences and other profoundly transcendent moments—before, during, and after working with their intuition and developing their Knowing. Be ready for anything, and keep good notes in your Knowing Journal.

Your path toward your *own* Knowing means that you will rewrite and expand these definitions to fit you. As you do so, you'll be creating your own understanding that's as unique as you are.

The Messy Basement of Your Mind

Although your unconscious mind is packed with information at any give moment—ideas, thoughts, feelings, flights of fancy, random associations, fragments of dreams—it's not the same thing as your intuition or your inner wisdom. Think of your subconscious as the messy basement of your mind, and your intuitive Knowing as the uppermost window in a meditation room on the top floor, a finished attic with plenty of light streaming through the windows and skylights.

Through complex processes we still don't fully comprehend, under the right conditions, you are able to sort through and pull up from that basement exactly the bits of information and awareness that create Knowing Moments, those flashes of insight that often contain the answers to complex questions, or the seeds of them. With contemplation, those initial "flashes" can be developed into very profound guiding inner wisdom.

Meditate on This

Yes, yes, you've heard this before. Meditation is the key to mental clarity, and mental clarity is a critical step toward inner wisdom or Knowing. Without mental clarity—a clean mental basement—your sense of Knowing will be incomplete, inconsistent, and unreliable. As you clean up that messy basement through meditation and contemplation, your intuition will become more reliable. You can then consciously create the conditions that support Knowing, which you can deliberately call upon to address the issues you face in your life. You'll have a wise advisor at the ready, whenever you need insight: your Knowing Self.

As a result of building that connection to your Knowing Self, you'll be much more calm, centered, and clear. You will become unshakable, able to take anything in stride without losing your emotional or spiritual balance. You'll be in that centered state of calm, empowered confidence where your Knowing resides, which some people call inner peace.

If you struggle with meditation, and everyone does in the beginning, it's because your mind is more interested in poking around in the basement. It's busy remembering the past, imagining the future, thinking about the wounds you suffered, and dredging up difficult emotions to which you don't want to admit, such as anger and shame. Initially, all that futzing around in the basement seems easier. At first, it *is* easier because you're more comfortable with the mess down in the basement than with the experience of being fully present in the Now. With practice that will change.

Flea markets, garage sales, and treasure hunts are fun sometimes, but do you really want one in your mind? Every day? Wouldn't an orderly mind, an organized basement where you could find things quickly and trust that they're in good working order, be easier to manage? That's what the following meditation exercise will help you create: an uncluttered mind.

Clearing Up the Clutter

You will need an undisturbed 10 to 15 minutes for this exercise, so shut off your computer and your cell phone. Remove yourself from any other possible distractions (such as your family members and pets). Sit comfortably in a straight-backed chair resting your hands in your lap, or lie down with your arms comfortably at your sides. If you prefer to listen to music as you meditate, choose soft, slow instrumental music so that the words will not distract or influence you.

As you breathe in and out, consciously slow and deepen your breathing pattern until you begin to feel fully relaxed and just slightly sleepy. Take care not to fall asleep.

Now imagine that you are sitting in a meditation room on the top floor of a house in a finished attic. Lots of sunlight streams in from the many windows and skylights. The room has been decorated exactly in the way that makes you feel most comfortable and serene. The room is almost completely perfect—but not quite. Notice that there's a table in the room, just a few feet in front of you.

Pose the mental question, *What three items do I need from the basement to finish this beautiful meditation room and make it uniquely my own?* Allow your first impressions to drift up to you. You might see the items appear on the table, you may simply Know they are there, or you may find that not much happens. If you don't see three items, or if there are more, that's fine. Whatever you experience is just fine because you're learning as you go.

If you simply can't get the items onto the table for examination, imagine yourself on a journey into the basement of your mind. Step by step, you're headed downstairs, until you reach the basement door. Open it. Allow yourself to experience the millions of possibilities for a few moments—this is one very full basement. Now ask your own Knowing to show you to the exact location of the three items you need right now to finish off that meditation room upstairs. Collect the items, taking care not to worry about logistics. If your left brain starts commenting with advice, judgments, or complaints, remind yourself that everything will fit just perfectly.

Return now to your meditation room on the top floor. Examine the items you've retrieved from the basement. Pay close attention to their color, texture, use, and particularly to any associations to other people or experiences. When you feel comfortable, open your eyes, and gently orient yourself to your surroundings.

Immediately write down your impressions and recollections. As you do this, be sure to scan your body for any physical tension you may be holding, or that occurs while you are writing your impressions. Do you feel tightness, constriction, heat, coolness, pain, numbness, or something else anyplace on or within your body? What emotional responses did you have, or are now having? Do you feel joy, sadness, shame, elation, guilt, awe, fear, love, or something else? Do your best to describe what is going on in as much detail as possible. Record the gist of it now while it's fresh. You can always repeat this exercise later, or scan your notes and extend the experience.

For the moment, we're done poking around in the messy basement of your mind. Now it's time to take a look (so to speak) at the first foundation stone of intuitive style: Visual Intuition.

CHAPTER 3
VISUAL INTUITION
AND KNOWING

"Few are those who see with their own eyes and feel with their own hearts."

—*Albert Einstein*

I Saw My Wedding to Nick the First Time We Spoke

Linda, a college professor, had a visual flash of her wedding to Nick—a man she hadn't even met—the first time they spoke on the phone. She pushed this vision aside; with two teenaged daughters and a busy professional life, she had no intention of marrying a second time. Where had this wild notion come from, she wondered. But when they met for coffee the following week, she again "saw" herself married to Nick. This Knowing unnerved her so much she almost refused to go out with him a second time.

Linda told a colleague the next day that she'd met a new man and that soon they'd be going on a formal date.

"Hmmm, I get such a good feeling about you two," her friend said. "This is weird because I know you just met him, but I just had a flash of you dressed for your wedding. I really think you're going to marry him."

"You see it too, huh? I just met him yesterday," Linda said, sighing nervously. "But I Know we'll be married someday."

How Visual Knowing Operates

Linda demonstrates the most common type of Knowing: a strongly visual intuitive style, sometimes called clairvoyance. As people vary, so does the way their visual intuition or Knowing operates, but three common "delivery systems" for visual Knowing are:

1. Through flashes of Knowing, which may be seen in color, black and white, sepia tones, or mini-movies.

2. Through dreams with particularly vivid or powerful imagery.

3. Through other outside images, often reflected repeatedly. An example is a pattern of numbers with significant meaning to the viewer, such as 717 to represent July 17, the birth date of a deceased loved one.

It's Not Your Imagination: It's Your Right Brain

The key to working with your visual intuition is to understand that it's not your imagination, and it's not your mind at work exactly. It's your right brain. Your visual intuition creates pictures with meaning from the cues the world brings you. Although the cues are important, it's where your right brain takes you, what associations you make, and what meaning you ascribe to the experience that evidences your Knowing. And it's found right there, in the right hemisphere of your brain.

Recently, at Drexel University in Pennsylvania, researchers using brain scans have associated flashes of insight while subjects solved word puzzles with the right temporal lobe, that processes metaphors and jokes. Some subjects had flashes of insight which allowed them to solve the puzzles quickly, whereas others took longer using more traditional logical methods to deduce the answers.

The researchers also found that right before the Aha! or Knowing Moment when the word puzzle was solved in an intuitive flash by some subjects, the brain stopped sending visual signals to its right temporal lobe. Researchers believe this may be the right-brain equivalent of closing one's eyes to better concentrate.

My sense—my own Knowing—is that eventually visual metaphors and visual Knowing will be found operating in that same portion of the brain. Interestingly, the temporal lobes are known to be the seat of mystical experiences such as out-of-body experiences and near-death experiences.

So, is your logical left brain feeling better now, knowing that the temporal lobe of your right brain is the root of much of this activity and that you're *not* "making it up"?

"Making it up" is imagination, which doesn't just strike seemingly out of the blue, as Knowing Moments do. You tell yourself, *It's time to take a mental break* or the pressure or the boredom builds. Soon you're looking out the window to daydream. Thinking—or pondering, mulling over, ruminating—also takes mental focus and feels like "work." In contrast, the imagery of visual Knowing is just there—boom—like that lightning flash of insight researchers are documenting in the right brain, or like the vision of Linda's wedding day was for both her and her colleague.

Researchers have repeatedly documented that we take in about 80 percent of our information about the world through our sense of vision. But when it comes to Intuitive Style less than 80 percent report it as one of their two strongest styles of Knowing (although it still tops the list). This is because much of the time, vision is a distraction to our quest for inner wisdom and Knowing. This may be why many of us reflexively close our eyes during meditation, contemplation, prayer, or when we want to be sure to pay attention to the spoken word, the feeling, or some other aspect of any experience.

The Visual Feast

Other people thrive on the powerful input of color, form, texture, and other aspects of the visual feast that is available at any given moment. Many of those who evidence very strong clairvoyant or clear-seeing tendencies report that they "see" even with their eyes closed. Surprisingly, this non-ordinary sight is found in those who are visually impaired as well. A study of blind near-death experiencers published in 1998 by researcher Kenneth Ring documented what he called "transpersonal vision." In the midst of a powerful spiritual experience, even people with no optic nerves could "see." They often had no context—what does red mean if you've never seen it?—but were still able to describe relevant details, such as the pattern of a man's tie.

So, even if you think you're not particularly visual, you might be surprised to discover that your intuitive style has a strong visual component. And even if you are very artistic or visually detail-oriented, you may discover you rely on other ways of Knowing much more than you realized.

Your Natural-Born Visual Intuition

The Visual Intuition Appraisal is part one of the Intuitive Style Inventory. Over the next several chapters, we'll build a comprehensive map of your Knowing by developing your Intuitive Style Profile, building block by building block. Let's begin by assessing the Visual Intuition component of your natural Intuitive Style.

Just respond quickly to the following questions. If you're not sure, respond anyway; there are no right or wrong answers and this is not a test. High scores are not better than lower ones, and your profile results should not be compared with others (unless you want to assess the intuitive talents of a group or work team to see what the team's preponderant style is). This journey into Knowing is all about *you*. This exercise is simply a way to help you better understand the visual component of your unique intuitive style.

How to Take the Visual Intuition Appraisal

Read each item below, and circle or highlight the number that seems closest to the truth for you.

- ✳ **Circle 1** if this statement does not apply to you.
- ✳ **Circle 2** if this statement applies once in a while, but not usually.
- ✳ **Circle 3** if this statement applies sometimes.
- ✳ **Circle 4** if this statement applies pretty regularly.
- ✳ **Circle 5** if this statement applies often.
- ✳ **Circle 6** if this statement applies most of the time.
- ✳ **Circle 7** if the statement applies all the time—or almost.

Visual Intuition Appraisal

1. I'm a very visual person.   1 2 3 4 5 6 7

2. I respond intensely to what I see.   1 2 3 4 5 6 7

3. I'm artistic (or am often told I am)   1 2 3 4 5 6 7

4. I easily remember people's faces and/or
   details of their appearance.   1 2 3 4 5 6 7

5. I have good color sense (or am often told I do)   1 2 3 4 5 6 7

6. When I recall important times in my life,
   I see pictures in my mind, or a movie-like
   image playing.   1 2 3 4 5 6 7

Total, Visual Intuition Appraisal: _____

Now add up your scores for each section. The lowest possible score is 6, the highest is 42. Double-check your addition before recording your scores in your Knowing Journal and on the Knowing Self-Portrait found in Appendix A.

Right now, your Visual Intuition Appraisal score will have relatively little meaning because it stands alone. As you complete other aspects of your Intuitive Style Profile in the chapters to follow, it'll make more sense. For now, here's a quick chart to help you understand where your Visual Intuition ranks in your toolbox of Knowing methods.

Visual Intuition Appraisal Score	Interpretation
40 to 42	Extremely Strong
37 to 39	Very Strong
34 to 36	Strong
28 to 33	Moderate
22 to 27	Weak
16 to 21	Very Weak
Less than 15	Extremely Weak

A score of 40 or higher means that you respond extremely strongly to visual data, whether you previously realized it or not. People who score at 37 or more on this dimension of Knowing usually follow guided meditations that have strong visual content quite easily. They have no problem "seeing" that relaxing beach scene or twisting mountain path. Such highly visual intuitives may find music played during meditation distracting rather than encouraging of a deeper state of relaxation.

Those who score in the lower ranges of Visual Intuition—27 and less—are the folks who struggle to "see" images during guided meditations. No matter how many times they listen to a meditation, they simply can't see the colorful rainbow or the bridge to the Other Side. Many of these folks have shared their frustrations with me: they feel like they've "failed" at something as universal as the ability to meditate.

Not to worry. If you're one of those not-so-visual intuitives, you're in good company, and you have other strengths in your Intuitive Style Profile. Remember that this is not a test or a judgment. Lower scores do *not* mean you are lacking in intuition, only that your Visual Intuition is not your most natural mode of Knowing. The process of Knowing and the way to your inner wisdom is as individual as you are, after all.

Following are some Inward Journey exercises to help you enhance whatever degree of Visual Intuition you already evidence. You'll also find some Power Points exercises designed to give you immediate feedback to see how well your intuition training is going. Seeds of Success practices show you simple ways to maintain your focus on the goal of developing reliable inner wisdom— your personal Knowing way.

✳✳✳✳

Inward Journey Exercise 1:
A Way With Words

Circle or highlight five words from the list that follows that evoke a response in you. Don't think about this—just respond intuitively to the words that seem to "jump out" at you.

Clouds	Music	Water
Painting	Sunset	Chair
Inside	Tree	Wind
Mountain	Car	Fire
Bird	Rain	Photograph
Conversation	Book	Snow
Dance	Outdoors	Beach
Deer	Night	Home
Sky	Animal	Lamp

The next step is to analyze the five words you chose (if you chose a few more or a few less, that's fine). Were you drawn to words that reflected people? Nature? Movement? What pattern do you see in your responses? Write this information down in your Knowing Journey Journal; you'll want it later.

Inward Journey Exercise 2:
The Rest of the Story

Now, take the five words you selected in Inward Journey Exercise 1, and use them in a story. You can do it; just make up a quick story of a few sentences, right now. Talk out loud or sketch your ideas on paper if it helps you. If you're stuck, begin with that old reliable, "Once upon a time there was...." Let your imagination go.

This exercise helps build your personal symbol dictionary for your visual intuition and can lead you into some very interesting, sometimes even profound associations and memories. As before, record this information in your Knowing Journal or in an audio or digital voice file for later reference.

Inward Journey Exercise 3:
Inner Artistry

You might want to put some lively music on for this one. Find some pens, pencils, crayons, markers in a variety of colors and some blank paper. The larger the better, but standard computer paper will work just fine. Choose an area of your life in which you'd like some guidance. Mentally (or out loud) say something like, "I bless you as an oracle of divine guidance and consider you a pathway to my visual inner Knowing. Please show me what I need to understand about this situation now." Create a statement in your own words to feel even more strongly connected to the exercise. After locating the rough center of your paper, close your eyes, grab something to write with, and let your hand go free. Don't worry about drawing something specific. It's best to just scribble and scratch anywhere on the paper that feels right. When you feel prompted to change colors or tools, do so. When you feel ready to stop, do so.

Now take a few moments to study your creation. Stand about six feet away, and review it from all directions. Move the top edge one-quarter turn to the right, then again so the original top is now the bottom, and so on. As if you were looking up at clouds, make notes of what patterns emerge and what thoughts, memories, and associations are evoked as you look at the image. Record this information in your Knowing Journal.

Inward Journey Exercise 4:
Smoke Signals

Smoke and fire have long been used in sacred ceremonies in churches, temples, synagogues, and mosques as well as in rituals of divination. For this exercise in smoke reading, select a candle that has an easily accessible wick. A taper style candle at least 8 inches tall will work nicely. Make sure that it is securely fastened in a holder and place it in a location where it is safe to work with an open flame. Keep a pitcher or basin of water nearby and do not allow children to conduct or participate in this exercise. This exercise should be performed in a well-ventilated area equipped with appropriate safety devices such as smoke detectors. You may prefer, as an extra precaution, to perform this exercise outdoors.

Next, find some plain, unlined paper (white works best). Avoid computer printer paper as the chemicals used to make it brighter will cause it to burn quite easily. Paper with some cotton content is better, although construction paper will also work, as will manila filing folders cut in half.

Choose an area of your life that you'd like some guidance about. Mentally (or out loud) say something such as, "I bless you as an oracle of divine guidance and consider you a pathway to my visual inner Knowing. Through the smoke patterns I am about to create, please show me what I need to understand about this situation now." Create a statement in your own words to feel even more strongly connected to the exercise.

Now, very carefully hold the paper over the very tip of the candle flame and move the paper slowly over the flame. You will find the best results occur when the paper is quite close to, or even just barely in, the tip of the flame. At this point, the paper will take on a soft glow like an oil lamp in a window. Take care not to burn a hole or allow the paper to catch fire. Continue to move the paper around and allow the smoke to create patterns on the paper. When it feels right to stop, do so.

Now hold the smoke pattern before you and see what images, impressions or pictures strike you. Stand about 6 feet away and see what pictures you see now. Turn the paper so that each edge is placed on the top and observe the smoke drawing from all four directions. Take notes on your impressions and what emotions are evoked in you as you do this exercise. If you'd like to keep your drawing, use a fixative spray from an art supply store to preserve it. Do not create more than two or three smoke impressions in any one sitting. This is an excellent exercise to repeat about once a week, particularly if you keep the drawings, date them and watch for repeated themes and patterns over time. (I always see birds and other winged creatures, no matter how many months or even years pass between the smoke drawings.) This is also an excellent exercise for groups because often others will see images you didn't notice.

Make notes about your experience conducting and interpreting smoke drawings in your Knowing Journal.

Power Points Exercises

These short exercises are designed to give you immediate feedback as you practice with your visual intuition. Move quickly when you do these to avoid letting your judging, rationalizing, interpreting left brain become involved. The goal is to use your intuitive, creative right brain.

Power Points Exercise 1: Go-Stop-Caution

Frame a yes-no question that relates to a decision over which you have full control. Decisions that are dependent upon the choices of others are not recommended for this technique (so "Will he break up with me?" is not a question to pose in this exercise). The decision should be something that isn't terribly "high level" or stress-inducing. The goal is to create opportunities to learn to use and practice with your visual intuition. Keep your questions straightforward and choose things that do not stir up strong emotions. An example of a question that would work well with this technique is, "Should I go to the movies Saturday?"

Now in your mind's eye imagine a standard traffic light that displays red for stop, green for go, and yellow for caution. If you struggle with seeing this in your mind's eye, download a picture of a traffic light from the Internet or find one in a magazine and study it until it "imprints" on your mind's eye.

Close your eyes. Mentally (or out loud) say something such as, "I bless you as an oracle of divine guidance and consider you a pathway to my visual inner Knowing. Through the colors red, green, and yellow, please guide me in this decision." Create a statement in your own words to feel even more strongly connected to the exercise.

Pose your question and see what color the traffic light turns or what color flashes to your mind. Just like a traffic light, red means stop or no, green means go or yes, and yellow means proceed with caution. As you're used to doing by now, jot down your experiences and reactions to this exercise, as well as any emotions it evokes in you in your Knowing Journal.

Power Points Exercise 2: Create a Face

Allow about five minutes for this exercise. Sit quietly in a relaxed position, as if you were about to meditate. Close your eyes, and on the "screen" inside your mind, just behind your forehead, imagine a powerful Etch-A-Sketch or computer graphics program that can create whatever you tell it to, quickly. Just as if you were instructing a sketch artist in the creation of a picture to help find a missing person or a suspect, start to create in as much detail as possible the face of someone you know well. Use as much detail as possible. Get the hairline exactly right; add every shade, texture, mark, and line (yes, even those) that make this person's face so dear to you.

Afterwards, take notes about your experience and your reaction to it. Even better, try to recreate on paper the image of the face you created in your mind.

Seeds of Success

The following is a list of quick little affirmations you can use any-time to reinforce your visual intuition through the power of your intention and focus. Choose one or two from the list that follows that particularly resonate, and keep them near you. Write them on a piece of paper to which you can easily refer, or create a text-based screensaver for your computer. If you prefer, use the following suggested affirmations to spark your own creative juices and create a few affirmations that are uniquely your own.

* ✳ "My visual intuition is strong, clear, and accurate."
* ✳ "I am able to see into the heart of a situation through the cues my visual intuition shows me."
* ✳ "I easily understand the visual metaphors my visual intuition shows me."
* ✳ "I clearly see and clearly Know what is best for me."
* ✳ "My visual intuition is my good friend who loves me and offers me guidance."

Chapter 4

Visual Intuition
in Action

"Matter is energy. Energy is light. We are all light beings."
—Albert Einstein

Another clue to how important we consider visual input in making sense of the world in which we live, as well as in developing our inner Knowing, is the focus (so to speak) we place on our visual sense. An example is the long tradition of divination. Among the wide range of divination techniques are many that rely primarily on vision, whether the usual biological sort or the extended, spiritual variety.

Ancient techniques, still practiced in some parts of the world by shamanic practitioners in many cultures, rely on the visual sense combined with symbolic meanings to interpret signs in nature and animal sacrifices. Ancient oracles often sought wisdom from the gods through interpretation of reflections or visions seen in bodies of water, particularly naturally occurring ones such as ponds, lakes, and still pools near waterfalls. Others practiced scrying using a bowl of water illuminated by the full moon or reflected firelight, although natural sources of illumination were considered better choices for true wisdom. A modern variation of scrying emerged in the 1800s: crystal ball gazing. Though it's not as popular as it once was, many people today keep crystal balls for their aesthetic qualities. More familiar in Western cultures are divination techniques including face reading or physiognomy, palmistry, handwriting analysis, tea leaf reading, and spirit art. All rely strongly on a person's visual sense.

Physiognomy compares the two sides of a person's face for symmetry; particular facial characteristics are considered clues to underlying character traits. Palmistry and handwriting analysis also rely strongly on comparative techniques and a database compiled largely through empirical observations—observations strongly tied to visual input and rife with symbolic meaning. Tea leaf reading also relies on the interpretation of images made by clumps of tea leaves and the positions of oracular clues. (I've long wondered whether the original developers of the Rorschach inkblot tests were first inspired by an aunt or grandmother who consulted tea leaves for guiding imagery). In spiritual art, usually shortened to "spirit art," a medium creates portraits of deceased people or symbolic images that represent key elements in someone's life.

Systems such as the tarot, runes, and the wide variety of astrological techniques rely on symbolism and relationships between and among the cards, stones, and planets. All of these approaches use symbolic systems developed by others. For this reason I don't recommend them as tools for developing your own Knowing, although they can be interesting, helpful, and just plain fun. You can develop a very strong, reliable inner guidance that never requires you to learn something as complex as tarot or astrology. Why rely on someone else's symbolic lexicon and not your own?

My goal in helping you to understand your own Knowing is to help you work with your Visual Intuition on your terms, to dive into your own inner wilderness without external reference points laid out in the cards or runes, to travel without a map by your senses alone. Just as great inventors and explorers learned by stretching the limits of knowledge, I want you to indulge yourself in your own sensory experience. Only through a strong, foundational knowledge of your unique way of understanding the world, through your unique bodymind (the two are intricately connected, after all), can you really begin to Know.

Colorful Language Tells the Story

Speech patterns are rife with clues to our understanding of natural-born intuition. Among the first few phrases we learn when studying any foreign language is "I see." (Interestingly, another is "I know.") This is probably because we highly value our visual sense, and also because from infancy we are repeatedly told, "Look!" as our families point to the world around us. Unless we live with visual impairment, we also rely on our visual sense the most in any given day, from driving to reading to computer game playing to television viewing.

In modern western culture, we quite commonly use color references to describe moods and emotions. We say things such as "He's been blue lately," "She's really in the pink," "That green monster runs his life." Purple passion, red rage, green with envy, sunny disposition—you get the idea.

So, to further assess how well your Visual Intuition Scale Score fits you, test it out in the real world. Your goal here is to pay attention to how you use visual metaphors while speaking. You might find it helpful at first to document the speech patterns of others with whom you interact on a regular basis to get a sense of how to detect when you are using visual imagery in your speech. Notice whether a colleague at work says things such as, "I bet he wishes he'd *seen* that coming" or "I *see* what you mean" or other visual references frequently. If so, he may have a strong visual component to his intuitive style.

Now give yourself the same scrutiny, and jot down how many times during a three-day period you use the phrase "I see" or its variations. Pay attention to your use colorful language (not the foul kind; it doesn't count for inner wisdom development), as in "she seems blue today" or "there he is again, with another dark cloud over his head."

As you develop your own style of Knowing, you may at first find that most of your symbolic references come through your visual field. This makes sense because of our historical heavy reliance on vision. I suspect it's also the reason why people who are visually impaired are among the most perceptive I've ever met. Visually impaired people often have extremely strong intuition: They've had to work with the lesser-used senses to compensate to some degree for their lack of visual sight.

Visual Symbolic Shorthand

Much of clairvoyance or Visual Intuition (in fact, much of Knowing) is based on personal meaning, what I call Symbolic Shorthand, which is relevant only to you. Why? Because it's grounded in your life experience, which is uniquely yours. Recording the signs in the world around you—and believe me, there are many—is the best way to build your personal reference set of symbolic shorthand symbols, your personalized Knowing dictionary. This will be extremely useful as you continue to expand your Knowing, whether you use your sense of Knowing for yourself only, or share your impressions and insights with others to spark their own inner wisdom. As you continue to work with different foundational elements of your intuitive style, be aware of the leaps of logic and association that you make. Often, these are the roots of powerful symbols presented to you in shorthand form.

An example is seeing a particular type of bird that always reminds you of your grandfather. After first consciously noting the association (it's a good idea to note these in your Knowing Journal), each time thereafter that you see that particular species of bird, you'll be training your Knowing to use that symbol to represent the concept of grandfather. Noting and using your quick visual associations as shorthand meanings will help speed up your sense of Knowing.

What Came Next?

Other times, those very personal symbols are simply meant to cue you to blurt out something that has meaning for another person. That's why paying attention to the "what-came-next" phenomena is so important to developing your process of Knowing. We have a naturally tendency to want sequential events to form meaning, but often each individual element is meant to stand alone. Even so, there is always a thread of connection running through all the data received in the Knowing Zone.

For example, the word *tree* might spark in you a visual memory of seeing yourself playing on a tree swing at your grandfather's farm 30 years ago. Your Knowing thrives in that seemingly random, tangential chain made of stuff found in that messy basement in your mind that is where the symbolic logic patterns that emerge from the symbolism are yours and yours alone.

This is why I recommend that you use dream dictionaries sparingly, and only to garner a sense of broad, archetypal themes that recur. An example would be the dream of being chased by a monster. That's archetypal: a classic story of the human experience, replicated through many cultures throughout the world. Who the monster represents is yours to interpret using your Knowing.

Visual symbols of Knowing work much the same way as dream symbols. They represent information of two types: literal and symbolic (and just to keep it interesting, sometimes *both*). Let's say you sit down with someone to do a practice consultation to test drive your visual intuition (which is an excellent strategy; for online practice settings see the Web Resources listed on page 217). You immediately obtain a visual flash of a tree. Now, it's time to explore the meaning of that symbol to both you *and* the other person.

If the meaning of the tree is literal, what type of tree your Visual Intuition shows you may be relevant. If you're practicing with another person by presenting your Knowing to him or her, don't ask your client to make meaning out of that tree. Extending *your* Knowing is the goal here, not a game of 20 questions. Relying on the recipient to make your Knowing associations is just plain lazy. As asking your fitness trainer to do your crunches for you would be, it's completely illogical and ineffective if you want to make powerful changes.

To help build on your initial visual flashes, ask your Knowing Self for more information. Let's say you now become aware that the tree you initially flashed on is a very large, old oak. This gives you a bit more with which to work.

You can ask the person you're working with if he or she can understand the meaning of a more specific tree; in this case a large, old, oak tree. If the person were to then tell you that he lived on Oak Lane, a street lined with ancient oak trees, throughout his school years, you Know you are being taken back to that period of his life. The next image you visually flash on will probably be particularly relevant to the person's childhood school years. Again, always pay attention to where you just came from in this chain of symbols.

If, however, the person has absolutely no association to a large, old, oak tree, *but you do*, it's symbolic. In this case your own vision of your grandfather's farm is the key element that you must "translate." Now you need to discern whether the tree means "tree" or "farm" or "swing" or "grandfather" or something else. If it turns out the person you're reading for had a grandfather who held square dances in the barn on the family farm, you're really getting good!

Embedded Meanings
and the Knowing Zone

As your Knowing evolves and your symbolic reference set grows, you'll discover that the same image will have what I call *embedded meanings*: it will simultaneously stand for several things, each of which has meaning to the individual and often is linked to the other meanings you bring up (are you still with me?). Basically, embedded symbols are *both literal and symbolic*. They're layered with meanings.

Other times, symbolic meanings are as plain as day, but you may still miss the meaning, or be pushed away from your own Knowing because you're not "sure" or someone else says, "You're wrong." But you very well may be onto something. Always pay attention to your sense of Knowing. Don't be rude or pushy, but when you're in the Knowing Zone—you'll understand more about what it feels like as you develop other foundational building blocks of your Intuitive Style— always honor it, even in the face of adversity and detractors. It's tough, but do it. If you can't say aloud what you're feeling when you're in the Zone, write it down so you can refer back to it later: it may well be that you learn later that you were quite correct, but that your left-brain knowledge hadn't yet caught up with and verified your Knowing.

Missing the Obvious

Misunderstanding visual messages presented through your Knowing Self is not uncommon. Many years ago during a consultation, I saw a huge cross just over a client's shoulder and behind it, an older woman's beatific, glowing face, looking down through parting clouds as if she were peering in from Heaven. It was an absolutely lovely image.

Initially trusting my Knowing, I told my client that I had his mother with me from the Unseen World. I was wrong, he assured me (rather gleefully; his wife had been the one who dragged him to a consultation they elected to share). His mother was fine and had no chronic health problems. She was a very healthy 67 years old. Instantly, I began to doubt my own Knowing sense.

Unbeknownst to him until later that day, his mother had unexpectedly died of a heart attack at exactly the time he, his wife, and I were together in my office. I learned this a few days later when his wife called with the news, and to thank me for showing her husband that his mother was already adjusting well to her new surroundings.

In this case, I'd had a very clear message, but I'd ignored it. I'd been talked out of it, actually. The symbols were extremely clear. Let me show you how the chain of visual symbols worked in this case. The man's mother had *crossed* (from the large cross symbol) *over* (from the over-the-shoulder reference) into *spirit* (from the clouds parting that allowed her to look down from the spirit world).

The mistake I made was that I didn't trust my own Knowing fully. After, all, intuitives—as can doctors and people from every other walk of life—can be wrong, too. When we are, it's usually a failure of interpretation of the symbolism through which Knowing operates; it's like improperly or incompletely translating a foreign language phrase. Sometimes events that we have a sense of Knowing about are not yet known to the parties involved, as happened in this case. But believe me, if I ever see a giant cross over someone's shoulder again during a consultation, I'll Know the translation. That image is a permanent addition to my visual symbolic shorthand dictionary.

Denying your Knowing because knowledge hasn't yet evolved enough to document that you're "right" is a huge disservice to your Knowing Self. Working from your inner wisdom, your own Knowing, is not about being right, although that's gratifying on the level of human ego. The secret is to speak the truth as you understand it, with compassion—and without attachment to whether you're right.

Recently, a woman I'd met 15 years prior in a meditation circle told me that information I had shared with her from my sense of Knowing had led her to investigate and, finally, discover an entire branch of her family she hadn't known about. The woman's mother had not been the biological daughter of the man she'd always known as her grandfather, as they'd both been led to believe. In this case, being documented as "right" took 15 years. And it only happened because the woman's sense of Knowing kept pushing her toward this life-changing discovery. Although she trusted me, she trusted her own Knowing far more.

Trusting your Knowing is a process of learning to recognize the signs of your inner wisdom at work in your life. Think of it as a scientist who has a Knowing Moment and then spends decades searching for support for his new theory shown to him via his inner wisdom; the gap between Knowing and knowledge is often a difficult, lonely place to be.

It takes courage to trust your Knowing. It's uncomfortable to "sit" with information that can't yet be "proven." It'll feel as though you've gone far, far out on a limb at times. At other times you'll wish you could just say, "See, I told you so!" Resist that temptation. Remember: Knowing is not about being right, although having your accuracy documented is very helpful while you are learning. That's why I encourage you to work with Power Points, small ways of getting immediate feedback to show you when you're on the right track with your intuitive interpretations. Keep records of your successes and failures in your Knowing Journal. Pay attention to the patterns you see emerging.

The rewards of working with your Knowing may not always be obvious at first, particularly when you're "wrong." But as you continue to stretch and grow your intuition into a powerful, trusted force for good in your life, you earn the biggest reward of all: Knowing that you are helping others even as you develop a stronger bond to your own spirit, your own soul, your Knowing Self. You earn rewards only by taking risks. One of the biggest risks (and one with an even bigger payoff) is sharing your Knowing sense with others.

Inward Journey Exercise 1:
Expanding Your Visual Symbol Dictionary

Record the following words and short phrases on a tape recorder or other device, allowing about seven seconds between each term. Then, either alone or with a group, respond with the first association you have. Write down your impressions and any other relevant details about your visual flashes, your instant visual "Knowing Moments."

Love	Mother	Journey
Marriage	Son	Job Change
Father	Divorce	Pet
Daughter	Baby Girl	Pregnancy
Illness	Graduation	Military Member
Office Worker	Move/Relocate	Wedding
Romance	Extramarital Affair	Cancer
Heart Attack	Surgery	Alcoholic
Drug User	Business Owner	Vacation
Baby Boy	Home	Spouse
Death	Car Accident	Lawyer

If you work with a group on this exercise, compare your responses to see how your shorthand symbols for a given term compare. You'll be surprised how often people agree, and even more surprised by the interesting ways in which they disagree. For some reason, in the United States, pink for baby girls and blue for baby boys is almost universally reported, while the images for divorce and wedding range widely.

Inward Journey Exercise 2:
What Color Is Your Parachute?

With a nod to the famous book by Richard Bolles, *What Color is Your Parachute?* (Ten Speed Press, 2004), I offer this as a fun group exercise that will definitely surprise you. Get together a group of people, some of whom do not know each other well. Ask for a volunteer. Have that person stand or sit in front of the others for about 20 seconds, preferably against a white or light, neutral-toned wall. Ask the viewers to write down what color the person is, without speaking aloud, thinking about it, or editing themselves (as in, "Well, he's wearing a yellow shirt, so I can't say, 'he's yellow,' it's too easy").

To keep it simple, and more meaningful, use only the colors of the rainbow, which are also classically associated with the major chakras or energy centers of the human body: red, orange, yellow, green, blue, indigo/midnight blue, and violet. I learned the importance of this the hard way. Once a mediumship student, also an artist, said, "She's turquoise with a purple edge and silvery sparkles" about another student, which was lovely, although extremely difficult to compare with other responses.

Then, count the number of people who responded with each color. You will probably find that most of the time, a significant number of people will say the same color, and many more will choose a color just next to it on the spectrum R-O-Y-G-B-I-V (remember him? Shorthand for red-orange-yellow-green-blue-indigo-violet).

For example, eight of 14 might say red and another three orange about a particular person. That's 11 of 14, or 78.6 percent responding to a range of two colors that together represent just 28.6 percent of the spectrum, which is quite disproportionate. Evenly distributed responses would be two per color using a seven color spectrum and polling 14 people, not eight reds and three oranges. Remember, and reinforce to yourself and others, that there is no right or wrong answer. Remind the group members that what the color they chose means to *them* is what's important, although using an aura color interpretation guide may be helpful at first as you develop your own symbolic meanings for color (see Appendix F).

For some people, red might mean passionate but for others violet, as in "purple passion," may have more meaning. This exercise works best with at least a dozen people, up to as many as 100 or so. You can even try it online with a group. Then, you will have no visual cues so your results should be even more intriguing when patterns such as the one noted here emerge.

Inward Journey Exercise 3: The Numbers Game

Now try the previous exercise with numbers rather than colors. Use 1 through 9 only, and don't use 0 (besides being confusing, some people take being called a zero a bit too personally). Have each person sit or stand before the group for 20 to 30 seconds, then poll the group for their opinion of what number each person is. You may want to use a simple numerology interpretation to guide you as you develop your own internalized symbolic shorthand for the numbers one through nine (see Appendix F).

Power Points Exercises

Powers Points Exercise 1:
Speaking of Knowing

The next time you watch someone giving a live presentation, notice how the speaker's energy shifts and changes during the presentation. Try watching through half-closed eyes, or even with your eyes completely closed. See what shifts in your awareness. Pay attention to the symbols and associations you make while the speaker presents, as well as whether half-closed or closed eyes make it easier for you to see from your Knowing Self. Jot these new symbolic shorthand references in your Knowing Journal for future use.

Power Points Exercise 2:
The Meaning of Things

Hold an object that someone you don't know very well has used on a regular basis. Often metal objects such as jewelry are easier to sense. Just as metal conducts electricity easily, it also conducts vibration easily. Now, simply allow yourself to see mental pictures. Write down or record the associations you make before sharing them with the object's owner so that you can fully experience the Knowing Zone before getting caught up in the feedback loop of being "right."

CHAPTER 5

BUILDING BLOCKS: AUDITORY INTUITION AND KNOWING

"All great men are gifted with intuition.
They know without reasoning or analysis, what they need to know".

—Alexis Carrel (1873-1944)

I Knew This Was a Time to Pay Attention

Roberto was headed to a trade show to interest distributors in his latest food invention. He excitedly told his seatmate on the long flight to California about his new high-protein, low-carbohydrate pasta product.

"Do you need a Canadian distributor?" she asked, blurting out the question unintentionally, suddenly remembering her friend Marianna, a dietician and food broker based in Ontario.

"We just had a call about that yesterday," Roberto said slowly, surprise evident on his face.

Although caught off guard, Roberto trusted his inner voice, which had guided him in his business decisions for nearly four decades. Although he easily could have found dozens of Canadian distributors at the trade show, the next day Roberto called the friend of the woman he met on the plane, who had no other connection to the food industry and who he never saw again. Marianna reported later that her friend's call was recorded just seconds after Roberto's on her office answering machine.

"She's my choice for our Canadian markets," Roberto said. "I trust my inner voice when it comes to people, and I just Knew that the woman I met on the plane was someone to listen to, and that Marianna and I would work well together and we have for a few years now."

Sometimes Knowing evolves. It requires a person to trust that first step, which leads to the next, and the next. It's exactly that process of Knowing when to pay attention to his inner voice that has helped Roberto make millions as an entrepreneur in the food industry.

Here are three common ways people with an Auditory Intuitive Style Know things:

1. Through an inner voice, like Roberto, who admits he doesn't "hear" this voice with his ears but rather inside his head, telepathically.

2. Through an outer voice, like those who've reacted to the instructions given by a voice they may or may not recognize, only to discover they've been helped in some way.

3. Through other outside sounds, such as song lyrics that guide a person through a difficult time, or a snatch of a conversation which seems to have a powerful meaning at a decision point.

You might have heard the term *inner voice* and wondered if you're supposed to actually hear one. Maybe—but maybe not. Some people do hear what sounds like an actual voice advising them, while others find that a fully-formed thought or sentence is just there—bam (as TV chef Emeril would say). If you've ever found yourself saying just the right thing, wondering even as you're saying it "where's *that* coming from?" you've had a moment of auditory or hearing-based Knowing.

An auditory intuitive style as the basis of your Knowing is an incredibly powerful tool, if you can learn to let go of any worries or fears that you're "crazy" because you "hear voices." Remember the story of Joan of Arc, who followed through on what she heard and changed the fate of a nation. History is full of such accounts; many spectacular ones are recorded in sacred texts throughout the world. Hearing is known to be the last sense we hold on to in the very end stages of life, and people who survived long comas often recount having heard the voices of medical personnel and family members while comatose.

Be inspired by the example of these people who, hundreds or thousands of years ago, had the courage to honor their inner voices of guidance. If they could honor their auditory Knowing with far less cultural support than we have today, you can certainly give it a try. Take notes, write down outcomes. Become a trained observer of the data. Approach your Knowing style and process as a scientist. Over time, you'll discover whether your hypothesis, that you can and do Know things through an auditory style, is substantiated.

Your Natural-Born Auditory Intuition

The Auditory Intuition Appraisal is Part 2 of the Intuitive Style Inventory. Continuing from the Visual Intuition Appraisal found on page 39, and over the next several chapters, we'll build a comprehensive blueprint of your natural-born Intuitive Style, which offers you important foundational data about your way of Knowing. You'll create a two-point Natural-Born Intuition Code that will help you understand and further develop your unique style of intuition.

Just respond quickly to the following questions. If you're not sure, respond anyway; there are no right or wrong answers and this is not a test. High scores are not better than lower ones. Your profile results should not be compared with others (unless you want to assess the intuitive talents of a group or work team), because this journey into Knowing is all about *you*. This exercise is simply a way to help you better understand the Auditory aspect of your unique natural born intuitive style.

How to Take the Auditory Intuition Appraisal

Read each item and circle or highlight the number that seems closest to the truth for you.

* ✳ **Circle 1** if this statement does not apply to you.
* ✳ **Circle 2** if this statement applies once in a while, but not usually.
* ✳ **Circle 3** if this statement applies sometimes.
* ✳ **Circle 4** if this statement applies pretty regularly.
* ✳ **Circle 5** if this statement applies often.
* ✳ **Circle 6** if this statement applies most of the time.
* ✳ **Circle 7** if the statement applies all the time—or almost.

| Auditory Intuition Appraisal |

1. I easily remember conversations accurately, even a while later.   1 2 3 4 5 6 7

2. I learn best by listening, not reading.   1 2 3 4 5 6 7

3. I learn other languages easily, or would if I tried to.   1 2 3 4 5 6 7

4. I appreciate music and I need it in my life.   1 2 3 4 5 6 7

5. I'm a good mimic and pick up accents and dialogue well.   1 2 3 4 5 6 7

6. Thinking back on events, I easily remember conversations and music associated with those events.   1 2 3 4 5 6 7

Total, Auditory Intuition Appraisal: _____

Now add up your scores for each section. The lowest possible score is 6, the highest is 42. Double-check your addition before recording your scores in your Knowing Journal and on the Intuitive Style Profile found on page 195.

Right now, your Auditory Intuition Appraisal score will have relatively little meaning. As you complete other aspects of your Intuitive Style Profile in the chapters to follow, and add the results from your Visual Intuition Appraisal from Chapter 2, it'll make more sense. For now, here's a quick chart to help you understand where your Auditory Intuition ranks in your toolbox of Knowing methods.

Auditory Intuition Appraisal Score	Interpretation
40 to 42	Extremely Strong
37 to 39	Very Strong
34 to 36	Strong
28 to 33	Moderate
22 to 27	Weak
16 to 21	Very Weak
Less than 15	Extremely Weak

A score of 40 or higher means that you respond extremely strongly to Auditory data, whether you previously realized it or not. People who score at 37 or more on this dimension of Knowing usually follow guided meditations that have strong Auditory content quite easily. They have no problem "hearing" that celestial music or the sounds of animals and birds in the forest they're guided through. Such highly Auditory intuitives may find visual content described during meditation distracting rather than encouraging a deeper state of relaxation; they'd much rather follow the voice of the meditation leader or go more deeply into the music.

Those who score in the lower ranges of Auditory Intuition—27 or less—are the folks who struggle during guided meditations. No matter how many times they listen to a meditation in a workshop or on a CD, they simply can't stay focused on the voice or the meditation music. Many of these folks have shared their frustrations with me: they feel like they've "failed" at something as universal as the ability to meditate.

If you discover your Auditory Intuition is not your strong suit at this point, remember that we have three other types of natural-born intuition to work through in upcoming chapters. Don't fret.

Plenty of research documents that we are not, by nature, beings who listen well; it takes time, focus, and practice. Even as a child, your music teacher probably played the flute, then the violin, then the cello individually as you trained your ear to discern the distinct voice of each instrument from the initially cacophonic sound of an orchestra.

Remember that this is not a test or a judgment, and lower scores do *not* mean you are lacking in intuition, only that your Auditory Intuition is not your most natural mode of Knowing. The process of Knowing and the way to your inner wisdom is as individual as you are, after all. Give a few of the following Inward Journey and Power Points exercises a try to strengthen your Auditory Intuition. Whatever its current level, stretching yourself by using these techniques will improve the Auditory component of your natural-born intuition.

Inward Journey Exercise 1: Reaching Out

You may want to tape or digitally record this exercise for future reference and to record key elements of it into your Knowing Journal. Recall an influential person from your life, whose advice you'd feel comfortable listening to. If you have concerns about your career, for example, recall a former manager, living or dead, whom you respected but with whom you haven't connected for at least three years.

Create the sound of the person's voice in your memory, particularly any notable speech patterns or phrases you associate with that person. Out loud, pose your question or concern, as if that person were right in the room with you. If you struggle with imagining the person in room with you, pick up a telephone or cell phone and pretend that you're placing a call to that person. Then relax and listen to what your auditory intuition, in the guise of a trusted adviser with whom you've had successful dealings, suggests to you.

Inward Journey Exercise 2: Musical Memories

Recall a song with lyrics of which you are particularly fond. If you don't know them by heart, or would like to search for a different song for inspiration, visit an online lyrics site such as *letssingit.com* or *getlyrical.com* where you can search for song lyrics in many ways. Without the music playing, imagine the song playing in your mind. As it does so, pay attention to what images from your life are evoked. Include people, places, and events. Write this information down in your Knowing Journal. The images may become new entries for your Symbolic Shorthand Dictionary, so highlight the ones that evoke a particularly strong emotional response in you.

Inward Journey Exercise 3: Team Effort

Sit in a straight-backed chair or lie down. With lights low and only instrumental meditation music playing softly (or no music at all), take several deep breaths as you move into a relaxed, meditative state. Continue to breathe deeply. Without actually using your voice, mentally invite your spiritual guidance team, which helps you Know your way in the world to join you. Don't worry about who they are or what they look like; simply request the team of advisers most appropriate for you at this stage of your life. As part of this request, specifically ask for the highest and best level of guidance you are able to receive at this point in your life; as your life evolves, the guidance around you also evolves.

While continuing to breathe comfortably and deeply, let the spiritual guidance team advise you. Specifically request that they communicate with you through your Auditory Intuition channel. If you find that you simultaneously see images or feel sensations, that's fine. Take mental notes of those phenomena to write down in your Knowing Journal, and again request that you be advised on your Auditory Intuition channel. No matter how many times you shift to visual or sensory forms of Knowing, gently and persistently request that you be guided on the auditory channel. If you hear buzzing or very high-pitched whining noises, rather than voices, simply ask that the vibration be slowed down to the level of human capacity for understanding. Be persistent, be patient, and ask for what you want.

Remember that you are in control of your intuitive receptors. You can "turn on" or "turn off" any mode of receiving that you wish to. You are not at the mercy of the method those from the Unseen World prefer to use to communicate with you; they will be flexible in responding to your requests for a more efficient connection.

Keep in mind a message is only a message upon being received, so they need you as much as you need them for the process to work. Think of the process as an interactive dance between two levels of reality, your physical realm and their spiritual realm, which blend at the edges and can be accessed from either side. You can take the lead and show those from Unseen World how you prefer the dance to proceed. Developing awareness and taking control are the keys to Knowing.

As you "hear" with your mind's ear, remember the sounds and tones as well as the emotions evoked. Some of these sounds may become part of your symbolic shorthand dictionary, so after you return from this meditative journey, write down all that you can recall in your Knowing Journal.

Power Points Exercises

These short exercises are designed to give you immediate feedback as you practice with your Auditory Intuition. Move quickly because the goal is to learn to understand flashes of auditory intuition.

Power Points Exercise 1:
Psychic Caller ID

When you answer the telephone and it's someone you've never met calling you, no matter what the reason, allow yourself to reach out past their voice and "hear" who the person truly is, to Know him or her more deeply. You might hear words pop into your mind's ear as you do this. If so, jot them down for your Knowing Journal. Also jot down what qualities you sense about the person based on his or her voice. Try to avoid descriptive qualities such as young, old, female or male, and instead reach to a deeper level. Can you hear kindness, fear, illness, fairness, intelligence, weariness, joy, sadness, or something else in the person's voice? Use what Daniel Goleman termed emotional intelligence, directed through your auditory intuition, to get to a deeper level.

Power Points Exercise 2:
Affirm Your Auditory Insights

These are quick little affirmations you can use to reinforce your Auditory Intuition through the power of your intention and focus. Choose one or two from the following list that particularly resonate, and keep them near you. Write them on a piece of paper to which you can easily refer, or create a text-based screensaver for your computer. If you prefer, use the following suggested affirmations to spark your own creative juices and create a few affirmations that are uniquely your own.

✳ "My auditory intuition is strong and clear."

✳ "I hear guidance easily from the source of my Knowing whenever I request it."

✳ "Voices guide me from the highest and best levels to lift me to my highest and best level."

✳ "My inner ear is sensitive and hears clearly what I need to know now."

✳ "I clearly hear and clearly Know what is best for me now."

✳ "My auditory intuition is my good friend who loves me and offers me guidance."

Chapter 6
Auditory Intuition
in Action

"Think of yourself as an incandescent power, illuminated and perhaps forever talked to by God and his messengers."

—Brenda Ueland

When was the last time you were in a quiet place, completely alone, with only your own thoughts? Even when you are alone, or in meditation, you may choose that time to listen to music. To hear the wisdom of your Knowing Self is difficult in our noisy, distracting world. But listening with what psychotherapists call "the third ear" is worth the inward journey.

Using your auditory intuition and learning to access the still, small voice of your Knowing Self requires the ability to hear the quiet. And hearing the quiet requires the proper environment as a foundation. That means you'll probably have to make a few small changes to your life in order to "hear" your thoughts, insights, imaginings, and practical wisdom for your life. Knowing grows best in the quiet corners, and requires some tending, as does any part of a garden that you hope will grow to its full potential.

To make a corner for Auditory Intuition, you'll need to build some quiet time into your schedule, even if it's just 10 minutes before you climb out of bed in the morning, or those moments driving in the car, alone, when you can turn the radio off. Although the attention required for safe driving means you won't be focused 100 percent on your Auditory Intuition, the intent to stay aware of your Knowing throughout your day is a big assist.

As you work on your Auditory Intuition, continue to operate as a participant observer rather than a detached observer. Learn to look at—and in this case, listen to—your life as an interesting science experiment. Remember that your mind and your body, your right brain and your left brain, your instinct and your imagination are all intricately entwined.

Over time, you'll learn to hear your Auditory Intuition more clearly. At first that inner voice may sound like a whisper, a high-pitched drone, or clicks and pops in your ear, but with patience and practice you'll discover that you have developed a reliable Auditory Intuition that can eventually lead you to what I call Knowing Moments. These are the times when you feel completely centered, calm, and clear and the voice of your own Knowing is heard, wise, calm, and clear.

Keep in mind that just as your inner vision sees a different world through what is often termed your third eye, so too your inner hearing tunes into a different world than this Earthly World that we live in day to day. Your intuition sees and hears the finer, softer vibrations of the Unseen World just beyond this one. Just as an oscillator, spectrometer, or radio receiver picks up only a range of what's possible, so too are your ordinary hearing and ordinary vision, the senses you use in this mundane Earth world, limited in their receptive range.

As does any good scientist, as a participant observer, you must review the products of your endeavors and your conclusions, and consider alternative explanations. Take "log notes" about your process of experimenting with your auditory intuition in your Knowing Journal. As you work with your Auditory Intuition and your Knowing, deliberately ask yourself questions such as, "What is the source of that idea?" and "What would tell me that it's wrong?" Being both a participant and a careful observer further enhances your ability to Know by engaging you in structured procedures, the stuff your analytical left brain thrives upon.

Yet whenever you are immersed in your left brain, using it to analyze, structure, and assess, it's also a wise practice to include the particular gifts your intuition can bring. By doing so, you build a bridge from your left brain to your right brain. The result of the process is a centered, balanced sense of Knowing.

If you're not used to accessing your right brain and its creative potential, you may struggle at first. The goal is to allow your imagination to roam freely. Speculate. Play. Wander in your right brain, your creative and intuitive center. Author Brenda Ueland, who introduced the term *moodling* in her 1938 classic *If You Want to Write*, reminds us that "...imagination needs moodling—long, inefficient, happy idling, dawdling, and puttering." (And you thought you were just futzing around aimlessly, not tapping your muse.)

Speech Cues to Auditory Intuition

Many people inadvertently broadcast cues to their natural-born Intuitive Style through their speech patterns. Those with strong Auditory Intuition are your family members, friends, and colleagues who say things such as, "I hear you," "You can say that again," and similar phrases that reference the sense of hearing or the act of speaking. As a means of gathering observational data about the strength of your Auditory Intuitive Style, write down how many times during a three-day period you use the phrase, "I hear what you're saying," or its variations. Because in modern Western culture, the primary sense we rely on is visual, you may find that you use variations on "I see" much more. This is important data, too. The data from your own life experience regarding how often and under what conditions you use auditory speech references will assist you on your journey to discern, expand, and apply the auditory aspects of your unique way of Knowing.)

What Auditory Intuition Sounds Like

Here's an example of how Auditory Intuition operates. In this case, Anne did not honor her Auditory Intuition, which led to rather serious consequences.

> "My boss invited me to dinner with a client who was visiting. I heard that little voice inside saying that I should just go home, so I told him I didn't really want to go. But because I didn't have what I considered a valid reason for not going, just that voice inside me, I decided to make the client and my boss happy, and eventually agreed to go to dinner.

"As we were about to leave for the restaurant, I got a terrible headache. Usually when I get a headache it comes on slowly and becomes progressively worse, but this one just hit me like a ton of bricks. As I was driving to the restaurant, I was involved in a car accident which totaled my car.

"A little over a year later, the same thing happened to me a second time: I should have listened. I was debating whether or not to go to the hair salon after work. I needed a haircut very badly, and this was the only day that week that I could go. I heard that same inner voice telling me that I shouldn't go, and then the headache hit me again.

"I ignored the two signs, both my auditory intuition and then my Body-Based Intuition, which kicked in, I guess, because I didn't listen to the voice telling me to go straight home. Instead, I went to the hair salon, and on my way home I was involved in yet another car accident. The next time I get signs like these, I will listen to my intuition and just stay home."

Not every case of hearing a voice speak results in negative consequences as it did for Anne; in fact, these were *positive* experiences, which intended to warn her of problems, had she honored them. Like many people do, particularly women who struggle with the "disease to please," Anne first folded under the social pressure of her boss's request to join him and the client. Later, the pressure of time—and the desire to look good, a value our culture highly endorses—led Anne to ignore that inner voice a second time.

Be mindful as you examine your decisions. Ask yourself, *Am I folding under outside pressure, or do I feel an inward call to do this, Now?* Once you've determined if the pressure to act is externally motivated (pushed at you from others) or internally motivated (persistently, gently encouraged by your Knowing Self), you can make your decisions in a place of heightened inner awareness. You may still choose to go to a dinner you aren't excited about attending, but you'll do it from a place of Knowing. Your conscious evaluation of the tradeoffs is important for making wise choices. And keep in mind that as Anne discovered, a true Knowing Moment will have more than one component. Anne also received cues from her Body-Based Intuition through sudden, severe headaches. She's certainly added that entry to her shorthand symbol dictionary under the category of warning signs.

Auditory Intuition Sent From the Other Side

The following is an example of an Auditory Knowing experience that falls into the category of after-death communication (ADC), an experience estimated to happen to as many as 40 percent of all people (although not all are auditory interactions). The following "thank you" experience that Carol relates is one of the most common types of ADC.

"My father had passed over nine months prior. While I'd dreamt of him on a few occasions, and certainly believed that he was with me on special occasions like my daughter's high school graduation, I can't say I'd truly felt a strong, powerful sign that he was around. I was working in the garden, something he had always enjoyed, too. But on this occasion, I distinctly heard him call out to me, even though I am the kind of person you could set a bomb off next to when I'm concentrating and I wouldn't notice.

"He said, 'Carol, thank you, thank you for helping your mother last week,' just as if we'd been having a conversation over a cup of coffee. I turned around but of course he wasn't there, at least not in a physical way.

"It was definitely his voice, though. It came from above me and over my right shoulder, as if when he spoke he was standing behind me while I was kneeling and planting. And it definitely came from outside me, which caught me off guard for a second, because I know he's gone. I guess I thought if he was going to talk to me, it would happen inside my head, sort of a mental communication or telepathy. Then again, I wasn't exactly surprised, because it seemed so ordinary right then, like, 'Oh, of course, Dad's here.'

"I was definitely pleased to hear his voice, or whatever it was; it sure sounded like his voice. You see, last week I insisted on taking my mother to her doctor because she's had a bad cold hanging on for weeks; it just wasn't clearing up. I know she's an adult and can take care of her health on her own, but this time I insisted. I felt sort of guilty pressuring her like that, even arguing about it with her.

"I'm glad I forced the issue, though. They found that my
mom is suffering from pneumonia. She's almost 80, so that's
a very serious condition for her. I guess Dad came by to
thank me for that."

Another common type of Auditory Intuition or Knowing is the danger warning. Recently I was driving back from an oceanside resort where I'd participated in a weekend conference. The weather was typical of early spring, quite windy with spots of hard rain. As I drove along a highway with a 50-mile-per-hour speed limit, I took care to keep extra distance between my car and traffic ahead of me because of the driving conditions.

Then I heard a very clear voice, not one I recognized, say to me quite distinctly, "Change lanes now." I've had experience with this sort of guidance, although it usually doesn't feel as urgent as this did, so I reacted quickly. As I changed lanes in the wind and rain, I remained completely focused, confident, and strangely calm, as if time had slowed down so I wouldn't move too fast.

Seconds later, a 15-foot aluminum ladder, which previously could not be seen under the tied-down blue tarp of the extended-bed pick-up truck that had been in front of me, came flying out, turning a somersault in the high wind before landing just where my car would have been had I not changed lanes. I'm used to hearing guiding voices (although believe me, for years I wondered occasionally if I was psychologically disturbed), so I didn't even pull over to collect myself. I wasn't shaken in the least. Grateful, absolutely, but not surprised.

The more you learn to work with your inner wisdom and guidance, the less you'll be surprised by its effectiveness. It will become simply one more way of Knowing the world, one more way to build trust in your own experiences. That's why intuitive Knowing is a gift that grows stronger with experience, and more reliable with conscious use.

Embedded Meanings
and Auditory Knowing

To build that centered confidence in your Auditory Intuition, you need to understand the particular way it works with you. Just as visual Knowing uses richly textured symbols and associations to convey meaning, so too does auditory Knowing rely on the embedded, multiple meanings created by sound. Sometimes sound creates mental "pictures," so if that's the way your auditory Knowing works, be glad: you'll be receiving information on two channels at once, both auditory and visual. Just as Anne's headaches reinforced the voice she heard saying "stay home," your Visual and Auditory Intuition will reinforce each other, bringing a greater confidence level to your Knowing. That means that, as a participant observer, you'll be able to test out how well these two aspects of your intuition support and enhance each other. And if your Visual and Auditory Intuition don't work well together, you'll be able to determine which one is more reliable for you, and under what circumstances.

For example, when I'm in danger, I hear a voice; at other times, my Knowing is much more subtle and often quite visual, even reflected to me through the world around me by what my Body-Based vision is drawn to. I pay attention to where my eye wanders, what sounds seem to rise above the din, and so on. The subtle aspects of Knowing require us to pay attention.

Inward Journey Exercise 1:
Expanding Your Personal Symbol Dictionary

The following is a list of common sounds that you can actually tape or find clips of online that you can download to your computer, a digital audio file, or a CD. If you can't, just allow yourself to recreate having heard them as fully and completely as you can using your imagination. Listen to a recording of the sounds themselves, or the words read aloud. Feel free to add some of your own sounds to this list.

If you are listening to the sounds directly, allow about five seconds to respond to each one. Don't allow too much time or you'll start "thinking" rather than letting your associations form intuitively. If you are working from your mind's ear by having the names of the items on the list read aloud, give yourself about 10 seconds between each phrase. This provides the time you need to recreate the sound as vividly as possible. As you listen, write down what associations you form. Pay attention to your first impressions and associations. What links to what and the "order of appearance" is important. If a certain word or phrase conjures up several associations or links, write them all down in the order they come up for you. If a word or phrase leaves you "blank," that's fine; just make a note of it.

Bell	Ambulance	Baby's Cry
Whisper	Thunder	Cat's Meow
Hymn/Religious Music	Angry Shouting	"Happy Birthday to You"
Child's Laughter	Coughing Fit	Static
Office Phone Ringing	Train Whistle	National Anthem
Dance Music	Stereo or Radio Playing	Sporting Event
Screeching Tires	Sounds of Lovemaking	Cell Phone Ringing
Orchestra	Wedding March	Crackling Fire
Dog Barking	Airplane	Medical Equipment
Police Siren	Door Slamming	Ice Cream Truck

Inward Journey Exercise 2: Connecting Points

You might want to use a different color pen or a highlighter for this part. After a few days, review your notes from Exercise 1, where you listened to the sounds or imagined them vividly in your mind's ear. See what associations "jump out" at you. Write down the who, what, when, where, how, and why associations. For example, does hearing or imagining the sound of an ambulance make you think of a particular person? Who? What were the circumstances? When was this? How old were you? How did the situation turn out? Why do you suppose this particular association came to you now?

All this is valid information that makes your Knowing yours, and yours alone. By "mapping the territory" of your mind and how it connects information, you'll be able to understand its special language and use it to further develop and communicate with your inner wisdom—your Knowing Self—through your personal symbolic shorthand.

Inward Journey Exercise 3: Radio Daze

Music is evocative for many people. When you think back on your first romance, or some other significant event in your life, you may associate it with a particular song. Even today, you probably can easily remember a tune you associate to a particularly happy time in your life. Rituals associated with music also are deeply anchored. We might not recall who attended a loved one's funeral, or what clothing we wore, but there's a good chance we remember at least one musical selection from the event.

In addition, many people report that they feel that their loved ones come to them through musical interludes after they've died. My own sister, a year after her passing, made her presence known through a series of songs on the car radio. As my surviving sister and I and a friend drove up into the North Carolina mountains to spread her ashes, changing the radio station on the rental car at least five times, several songs from different musical genres played. Each one had a particular meaning to us. From the first lyric we heard ("With all my heart—Ya know I'll always be right there" in "I'll Always Be Right There" by Bryan Adams) right on through "Westbound #9" (a song about a bus by The Flaming Embers; my sister never learned to drive and used public transit to get around), we all Knew something powerful was happening. It was a joyous, laughter-filled day of celebration of my sister's life, which still ranks among the most special days of my life.

Music and Healing

The power of music in healing is well documented. Patients struggling with terminal cancer often find that music provides them welcome respite and emotional sustenance, helping them to journey beyond the struggles of the body. Alzheimer's patients are also known to respond to the music that was popular in their youth, despite often being unresponsive otherwise.

You too might find messages in music. Here's an exercise to try. As usual, keep a record of this intuition experiment in your Knowing Journal.

Allow yourself about 20 minutes for this exercise. Turn on a radio station you don't usually listen to so that you are somewhat unfamiliar with the music. If you know or can easily find out, note the song. As the music plays, draw or sketch what images come to your mind. If you aren't trained in art, don't worry; this is only for you. It's just data, not art. Just doodle. Move your hand around on the paper. Let your mind wander. Write down words that come to you as you draw. If you are still struggling to do this, try using your non-dominant hand (if you're left-handed, use your right hand; if you're right-handed, use your left hand) to sketch the images. Let your auditory Knowing channel connect itself to your hands, and sketch the result.

If you find this difficult, try again another time. Don't "work" at this, or any other intuition development exercise. Simply allow the information flow to you, comfortably and easily. Never force it.

In a few days, go back over your sketches and notes. Pay attention to what patterns emerge. Pay attention to whether the images you drew have different meaning now, or seem to be allude to something "bigger." Write down all your impressions and associations.

Pay attention to the process, too, not just to what you see on the paper. Think back: Did you sketch more during slower music, or faster music? Did you respond more to the lyrics or to the melodies? All this is useful data for the journey into your own Knowing, so don't worry about taking too many notes. Just as a scientist would, write up your results later in a few summary sentences or short paragraphs. Use this information to create the best conditions to access your Knowing Zone on demand.

CHAPTER 7
SENSORY INTUITION
AND KNOWING

*"How much do we know at any time? Much more, or so I believe,
than we know we know!"*

—Agatha Christie, The Moving Finger

My Wife Still Guides Me

William's wife Joan died after a seven-year struggle with two bouts of cancer. Since that time, he's discovered that his wife still supports, guides, and comforts him—just as she had for more than 40 years.

> "When I was wondering whether to sell our home and move to a smaller place, I felt her all day, as if she were walking through the house with me," William said. "I know this might sound strange, but she was right by my side. I could feel her energy, I guess; I'm not sure what to call it. But I have no doubt it was Joan. By the end of the day, I Knew selling the house was the right thing to do."

William also Knows that Joan has guided him to take better care of his health.

"I was thinking about Joan, looking at a picture of us on the beach from about 20 years ago, when the phone rang. It was my dermatologist's office, reminding me I'd missed my appointment the day before, and telling me they had a cancellation, if I could come right away," William said.

"I was just going to schedule an appointment for a few months later, because I was very busy with my business then. But suddenly I felt Joan with me, right in the room. My skin tingled, I felt warm, and I could smell her fragrance. I knew Joan was there, telling me this was important. So I took the appointment.

"They found something suspicious on my forehead and did a biopsy right then. It was skin cancer, pretty serious. I had surgery on it that afternoon. I Know Joan saved me from the kind of struggle she endured with cancer. I Know she guided me then," William said. "And she still does."

William is fortunate that his wife supports and guides him still. But despite her strong connection to him it was his *own* Knowing—primarily through is sensory awareness—that caused him to pay attention to what many people would dismiss as coincidence, luck, or synchronicity (also called meaningful coincidence). But because he took a chance and trusted his sense of inner wisdom, his skin cancer, which was severe enough to require skin grafting and plastic surgery later, was addressed in time.

Sensory vs. Gut/Body-Based Intuition

This and the next few chapters deal with two types of what is commonly called clairsentience, or clear-feeling. Because I've observed two distinct types of clairsentience, I've created two distinct categories of clairsentient intuition: Sensory Intuition, "skin-out" intuition, which can be very subtle; and Body-Based or "gut" Intuition, which is felt more deeply in the body, on a much more visceral level. Though both are technically forms of clairsentience, the distinctions between these two types of Knowing are important.

Sensory Intuition includes the ability to tune into what I call "field" energies as well as clairgustience (clear-tasting, such as suddenly "tasting" a food associated with a particular person or memory) and clairolfactory sense (clear-smelling, such as "smelling" pipe tobacco or perfume).

Being able to tune into the mood in a room, the distinct energy of someone who's passed, and feeling what are often called "ghosts," but which are more properly referred to as spirit beings to distinguish them from human beings, are also common aspects of Sensory Intuition. Sensory Intuition includes changes to the skin—flushing, temperature shifts, and goose bumps.

In contrast, Body-Based Intuition is much stronger and often its messages are confused so that a person, as Anne did in Chapter 5, feels that a headache is not an intuitive sign of Knowing, but a symptom of a health problem. Examples include "feeling" the pain of someone else's broken leg or the nausea symptoms of another person's pregnancy. In many ways, Body-Based Intuition is the ultimate empathic response: a person's body "mirrors" that of another as a way of offering sensory-based intuitive insights.

Many medical intuitives have very strong Body-Based Intuition, as do many nurses and other health practitioners, including practitioners of alternative health such as reiki and spiritual healers. Often, whether it's a conscious response or not, the "mirroring" is what guides an intuitive healing practitioner to focus on a particular area of a client's body.

Unfortunately, the powerful intuitive insights that our bodies provide are often dismissed. But with some conscious focus, these sensory insights can be developed into Knowing by the application of a structured approach to verify or expand the information using the other foundations of inner wisdom—Visual, Auditory, and Mixed Intuition. The goal is to use the body as a data-gathering tool and to, as dispassionately as possible, examine the data in a systematic way.

Among the most common ways that people evidence moments of Sensory Intuition are:

1. Feeling someone with them, although that person is far away or deceased.
2. Experiencing goose bumps on the skin, or any other skin-based response—a flush, a chill, or a sense of having been touched while alone.

3. Intuitively smelling a particular fragrance—a perfume, floral scent, tobacco or pipe smoke, or other notable scent associated with someone else who is not physically present.

4. Intuitively tasting a particular food associated with someone else who is not physically present.

Speaking of Sensations

Many people with strong Sensory Intuition say things such as, "I feel that we should..." and "My sense is...." For the next few days, as a means of gathering data about you, use sensory intuition and write down how many times you use sensory references in your speech.

Sensory Intuitive Style Traits

People with strong Sensory Intuition tend to be very sensual in many areas of life. They like affection and often have strong sexual urges. They appreciate the tastes and aromas of well-prepared food. They often enjoy movement such as dancing and sports. They're the ones who say things such as, "Whatever I wear must feel good against my skin. It's got to be comfortable."

How to Take the Sensory Intuition Appraisal

Read each item, and circle or highlight the number that seems closest to the truth for you.

* **Circle 1** if this statement does not apply to you.
* **Circle 2** if this statement applies once in a while, but not usually.
* **Circle 3** if this statement applies sometimes.
* **Circle 4** if this statement applies pretty regularly.
* **Circle 5** if this statement applies often.
* **Circle 6** if this statement applies most of the time.
* **Circle 7** if the statement applies all the time—or almost.

| Sensory Intuition Appraisal |

1. I am a very feeling, emotional person.   1 2 3 4 5 6 7

2. I can tell when someone enters the
   room, even if he or she makes no sound.   1 2 3 4 5 6 7

3. I have felt strongly that someone I know is
   with me, even though he or she was at a
   geographical distance, or have died.   1 2 3 4 5 6 7

4. The layout, lighting, and color scheme of a
   room strongly affect me.   1 2 3 4 5 6 7

5. People tell me I'm compassionate and empathic.   1 2 3 4 5 6 7

6. When I recall important events, I can easily
   remember the mood or feeling, almost as if
   I'm reliving it.   1 2 3 4 5 6 7

Total, Sensory Intuition Style: _____

Now add up your scores for each statement. The lowest possible score is 6, the highest is 42. Double-check your addition before recording your scores in your Knowing Journal and on the Intuitive Style Profile found on page 195. Your Sensory Intuition Appraisal score will have greater meaning as you complete the Intuitive Style Profile. If you want to move quickly through the Intuitive Style Profile sections and return later to the development exercises for each type, see page 39 (Visual Intuition Appraisal), page 60 (Auditory Intuition Appraisal), page 80 (Sensory Intuition Appraisal), page 98 (Gut/Body-Based Intuition Appraisal), and page 115 (Mixed Intuition Appraisal).

Sensory Intuition Inward Journey Exercises

To sharpen your Sensory Intuition, give a few of the following exercises a try. Let your intuition guide you to the ones that seem right for you at this time. Be sure to take notes of your experimentation process in your Knowing Journal; you'll use the themes and patterns that emerge later.

Inward Journey Exercise 1:
Feelin' the Vibes

When interacting in a situation where you don't know everyone present, such as at a party or on an airplane, take a moment to sit quietly, out of the main action as much as possible. From your position on the sidelines, close your eyes and just allow yourself to feel the energy of what's going on nearby. Does the "vibe" feel happy? Tense? Agitated or angry? Joyful? Phony? Bored? Practice with your eyes open, too, and see if you can sense better with your eyes open or closed. Neither one is wrong—just choose what works best for you after experimenting with both techniques.

Also create a shorthand code symbol or word you can use to note whether someone is being consistent (their inner mood matches what their outer demeanor broadcasts, they're being authentic) or inconsistent (their inner mood does not match what their outer demeanor broadcasts, they're being inauthentic). This shorthand code will soon become internalized so that when you meet new people, your initial impressions will become more accurate and your Knowing sense more trustworthy and reliable.

By now you probably realize the value of keeping track of your impressions, both of the process and of the results. Just as a scientist keeps a log of his experiments to learn what works and what doesn't, you'll discover that logging your progress guides you in what works and what doesn't for your *own* Knowing, which is unlike anyone else's (so comparing notes won't help much, although it's fun).

Inward Journey Exercise 2:
Animal Essence

This exercise guides you into resonating with the field energy of an animal. Whether you choose a dog, cat, fish, ferret, bird, lizard, an animal in the wild, or at the zoo, be ready to experience new levels of understanding. Most people initially find that conducting this exercise with mammals works best, probably because humans are mammals, too. Keep practicing and, one day, you may become your own "pet psychic" just by tuning in through your sensory intuition.

If possible, sit across from or hold the animal with which you wish to commune. Ideally, you should be positioned so that you can look into the animal's eyes (but be careful: Many animals will interpret a steady gaze as a threat and may attack). Some people, however find they glean more information though closed eyes. Try the exercise both ways, do what feels most comfortable and, yes, jot down what you learn from this experiment.

If you can do so comfortably, try to match your breathing rhythms to the animal's. This is not always possible, so at least do your best to take an inward breath when the animal does; the goal is to become consciously synchronized with the animal's world as much as you can.

Now, allow yourself to resonate with the animal's energy field. What does it remind you of? Is it soft? Prickly? Frightened? Trusting? Wounded? Pay attention to all the sensations you feel, particularly those on your skin. Where do you feel an itch? Where do you instinctually want to place your hand for comfort? Try to "shrink" or "expand" your energy field so that you feel as small or as large as the animal with which you're conducting the experiment.

Pay attention to all the bodily sensations you feel—hunger, thirst, body temperature, leg positions, and so on. If you like, mentally pose a question; something open-ended such as, *What should I Know about you Now?* is a good choice. See what impressions, sensations, visions, or sounds you experience in response. If you like, take a few moments to send energy, thoughts, or information you'd like to share to the animal. After you complete the exercise, write down both your responses to the process as well as any insights you gleaned.

A variation on this exercise is to work with a plant or tree. Most people find that this inward journey is easier with animals initially, but powerful aspects of your own Knowing can be enhanced by working with other aspects of the natural world. You might also like to try working with a photograph or other image of an animal.

Inward Journey Exercise 3: Reality Testing

Tune into a "reality" television program for an episode. This is an experiment in accessing your own Sensory Intuition, an aspect of your Knowing, so it doesn't really matter too much what program you watch. Your goal is to witness one person in the program and sense his or her underlying character traits and patterns, which generally are obscured by the contrived situations which are the basis of reality television programs.

Select an individual to whom you have an immediate, strong emotional response, either positive or negative, to follow for one or more episodes. Keep your Knowing Journal close at hand for note-taking. Consider the person on the television program the "sender" and you the "receiver" in this interaction. First, pay attention to the way your body responds to this individual. Notice particularly how your skin feels. Where do you feel itchy or want to move your hand? What temperature fluctuations do you feel? Is your face hot or cool? If you have a tough time assessing this, make a deliberate section-by-section mental body scan, starting at your feet and moving up your body to your head.

Next, pay attention to the "field" around the person you've chosen to watch for this experiment. What emotional responses do you feel? Are you angry? Happy? Calm? Edgy? Sad? Worried? Write your feeling responses information down in your Knowing Journal.

Now, quickly choose five words to describe this person. Don't worry about being right or wrong. Just become comfortable with your *own* process of sensing the other person's energy. This is about developing good antennae. Later, in a final episode of the reality program, or in follow-up interviews, you may be able to verify your impressions based on the views of others who interacted directly with the individual you chose to watch ("Yes, the whole time we were on the island he was a big…"; "We were all pleased when he said 'you're fired' because she was…"). If you are able to gather such data, just add it to your Knowing Journal. It may seem like gossip on one level, but it's actually helpful information that can guide you in better understanding your Sensory Intuition and enhancing what Daniel Goleman named emotional intelligence.

Power Points Exercises

Here are three quick ways to tap your sensory intuitive talents. You Know by now to take notes for future reference.

Power Points Exercise 1:
Read the Scene

As you enter a new environment where you will spend at least a few hours, such as a hotel room or a table in a fine restaurant, extend your sensory intuition to tune in to the "vibes" of the person or people who were here before you. Again, you won't have a chance to verify if you're "right" or "wrong" and it doesn't really matter. The goal is for you to sense what "tense" feels like to you, compared to, say "loving," without the need for external verification. This is, after all, an inward journey.

Power Points Exercise 2: Color Cues

Cut up several colored construction papers sheets, and place a single small piece (maybe 2 x 4 inches) in an envelope that cannot be seen through. Create three or four envelopes with the same color in each; use at least five different colors so that you have 15 to 20 sealed envelopes. Have someone else number the envelopes sequentially so that you have no idea what numbers correspond to which colors. Shuffle the envelopes so that the colors are mixed well. Select an envelope. Sense what color you feel is inside, and write the number and color down on a tally sheet. When you have gone through all the envelopes, open them and see how well you did. Don't worry if you failed miserably—your goal is to extend your sensory awareness so you can't fail, actually. Later, you can work on accuracy.

This is an excellent exercise to do in small groups. A mix of adults and children will quickly show you that children are very good at sensing colors. Their success in this task will cause them great delight as it's rare for children to be more skillful than their elders in anything. Indulge them, and while you're at it, pay attention: what is it that the children are doing that the adults are not? In a word: trusting. Their left brains aren't developed enough through the educational process to completely discount their right-brain-based intuitive impressions.

As you do this exercise, whether alone or in a group, pay attention to your body's signals, which may be very subtle. Many people notice that they feel a "tingly" sense corresponding to the chakra system. Red will be sensed low in the pelvis, yellow just below the waist, green in the center of the chest near the heart, blue in the throat area, and so on. Whatever you feel (or don't feel), be sure to write it down in your Knowing Journal. You are gathering data for evaluation, so your frustrations, as well as what you find difficult and what works easily, are insightful clues about how your Knowing operates.

Power Points Exercise 3:
Seeds of Success Affirmations

Use the following affirmations anytime to reinforce your sensory intuition through the power of your intention and focus. Choose one or two from the following list that particularly resonate, and keep them near you. Write them on a piece of paper to which you can easily refer, or create a text-based screensaver for your computer. An even better approach is to use the affirmations to spark your own creative juices and develop affirmations which are uniquely your own.

* ✷ "My Sensory Intuition is strong and easy for me to understand."
* ✷ "I am able to comprehend the truth of a situation through the cues my Sensory Intuition provides me."
* ✷ "My Sensory Intuition blends comfortably with my other intuitive senses, my intellect, and my emotions to provide me with useful data about any decision with which I am faced."
* ✷ "I clearly sense and deeply Know what is best for me and I act on it, carefully and wisely."
* ✷ "My Sensory Intuition is my good friend who loves me and offers me guidance."

In the next chapter, we'll move from the theoretical to the practical by considering how Sensory Intuition operates in the lives of real people—and what could make it stronger and more reliable tool for living.

CHAPTER 8

SENSORY INTUITION
IN ACTION

"The best and most beautiful things in the world cannot be seen,
nor touched, but are felt in the heart."

—Helen Keller

The brain and body, which more and more we are coming to view as a unified system, are designed to protect us. The survival instinct is the strongest of any that we have. Scientific researcher and author Candace Pert, Ph.D., suggests, in her groundbreaking work *Molecules of Motion* (Scribner, 1997), that the body is comprised of "molecules of emotion," which essentially give it "brains" in many places. The way Sensory Intuition (one aspect of Knowing) operates reinforces that concept.

Of the five basic building blocks of intuition—Visual, Auditory, Sensory, Gut/Body-Based, and Mixed—it's Sensory Intuition that people seem to most struggle with. Why? My theory is that we're used to relying on vision and hearing to get through our days. Of the five senses, these two are the workhorses. So, when we access Visual or Auditory Intuition, we tend to give it more weight than its more subtle cousin, Sensory Intuition.

Another theory I have for why we so discount Sensory Intuition is that in modern Western culture, we tend to deny our bodies on a regular basis; we simply don't pay attention. We say things such as, "No pain, no gain" when pain may be a signal to stop the abuse we are inflicting on our bodies. More than 2/3 of Americans are overweight, partly because we do not heed our bodies' natural signals that tell us we've had enough. Instead, we override the signals our bodies provide, and keep eating until the plate is clean, and the pounds pile on. We have become so disconnected from our bodies that we tend to completely overlook the wisdom they bring us, the Knowing we could glean, investigate, and perfect. I am certain that we miss information that would help us live better, more balanced, happier lives because we aren't paying attention to our Sensory Intuition. The better you understand your body's way of communicating, the better you are informed about everything that could affect it, from workplace stress and painful personal relationships to health concerns. Following are some example of times when the Sensory Intuition was so strong that people could not deny it—and trusting that Knowing improved lives for many.

Rebecca's Fatigue: A Sign to Add More to a Busy Life

Rebecca, a 37-year-old married woman with two children (Sarah, 9, and Michael, 6) was fatigued. Chronically fatigued. She was busy with two school-aged children and part-time work as a dental hygienist which occupied two (very full) days a week. Then there was her husband, Kevin, with whom she had a solid bond, complete with strong sexual chemistry even after 12 years of marriage. It all seemed perfect. But it felt quite different to Rebecca. She felt like she painted a brave face on every day, and tried to keep all the balls in the air, like a skilled juggler.

Rebecca had convinced herself—not without good reason—that her ongoing fatigue was the result of being a busy mom, wife, worker, daughter, and friend. But visit after visit to her internist and her gynecologist had left her, and them, baffled. Thankfully, Rebecca had no medical symptoms that pointed to a disease; even chronic fatigue syndrome wasn't the culprit.

Rebecca's logical left brain told her that her tiredness was the result of her overscheduled, frantic life. Her project-engineer husband, her working-mother friends, and her stay-at-home-mom friends all agreed with her left-brain assessment: Her ongoing fatigue was, essentially, the curse of a busy life in a modern era.

Although that seemed reasonable, Rebecca's frustration was mounting to the point where her internist's suggestion that she seek out a therapist seemed to be a good idea. In talking with the therapist, Rebecca realized that she had received many subtle clues about her dilemma over the years. Her hands twitched often, which she'd just considered a nervous habit. Her hands were very dry, and itchy, which she attributed to the effect of the gloves she wore at work. Sometimes she had a feeling of heat rising (probably perimenopause, reasoned her informed left-brain) when she was thinking about a career as an artist, something she'd dreamed of as a child, but had been talked out of because it seemed impractical.

Now, more than 25 years later, Rebecca realized, with the help of her therapist, that her body was paying the price for her unsought dream. Her fatigue was the result of a constant effort to suppress her soul's cry, to quiet her inner Knowing which had for decades been reminding her that art was her passion. The logical explanations, all of which made perfect sense, didn't consider what was going on in Rebecca's soul.

As much as she loved her life, by not expressing herself as an artist, she was denying a huge part of who she was. And that was the root of the ongoing fatigue. Rebecca began to take private art lessons in her home, and discovered within weeks that she was more energized than she'd been in years. She'd simply needed creative expression, not therapy, depression medication, or a sabbatical from her busy life.

✳✳✳✳

Through the process of investigation, in this case with the help of a trained outside professional, Rebecca figured out what her Knowing was calling her toward. Even if she never becomes a famous artist, her Sensory Intuition had been gently reminding her of and prodding her toward the process of creation. The symptoms of fatigue; itchy, twitchy hands; and the heat of what is called kundalini rising all reinforced a latent, unacknowledged Knowing in Rebecca. Her life was out of balance, and attending to creative expression would heal her through releasing her fatigue.

How do you discern what may be health problems and what may be your need to change your life? First, as Rebecca did, be sure to get good medical support to rule out any underlying health problems. Then, spend some time doing a life inventory that incorporates your Sensory Intuition. You'll find some good questions to begin with in Appendix C on page 201.

Ask yourself some key questions, and listen to what your body tells you. Don't make hasty or rash decisions about your life; as Rebecca did, take your time and explore. Your Knowing is a persistent, gentle force that will continue to prod you until you pay attention. If you deny it, its force gets stronger, but it doesn't "whack you upside the head." If you conduct a careful life assessment, you'll be able to look back and see that, had you been paying attention, you'd have been able to see the "whacks" of your life coming. This isn't what's been called 20/20 hindsight; this is a life review and assessment to better understand your body's sensory intuition.

Conducting a Life Assessment

As a participant observer, a researcher looking at your own life carefully, notice how you feel about different areas of your life. When you're with your children, are you fully engaged to the point where time seems to fly? Do you barely notice your body at all? If you're that much in the Zone with your kids, clearly your Sensory Intuition is reinforcing you in that role of parent.

Do you find yourself finding excuses to avoid your spouse or lover? That old joke that people say, "I have a headache" to avoid romantic encounters may instead be based on a Sensory Intuition that is saying, "I hurt around this person." That's your inner wisdom, your Knowing, asking you to pay attention.

Perhaps you avoid romantic encounters, letting your logical left brain convince you that you just don't have time, or that because you're older than 40, there's not much chance you'll find love. Remember that study that claimed a woman older than 30 had a better chance of being struck by lightening than of marrying? How many funerals for women struck by lightening have you been to, compared to weddings? Deep down, you Know that happiness will find you, if you put your intentions toward it and move past fear.

Well-known activist and prolific writer Audre Lorde reminds us, "When I dare to be powerful, to use my strength in the service of my vision, then it becomes less and less important whether I am afraid."

Take time to assess where you allow yourself to be powerful and where you allow yourself to be afraid.

Do you dread your workplace? Perhaps Monday morning finds you muttering while driving, "Just five days. I can do this. It's just five days." If so, you're receiving some very definite clues that something is awry. Your health will eventually give out, somewhere if you don't honor your body's intuitive wisdom. Put your sensory intuition to work as a means of accessing your inner wisdom, your Knowing. Pay attention to what resonates and just feels right as you assess your life circumstances.

Sensory Intuition in Matchmaking

Here's another example of how Sensory Intuition operates. In this case, Mark honored his Sensory Intuition, which led to a powerful life change.

"I'd always dated women who were, well, beautiful, basically. It wasn't that I ignored women who weren't obviously, almost aggressively attractive—well, okay, it is that I pretty much ignored women who didn't play up their looks. I always fell for the tall, blonde types, the ones that some other women, like my sister, Lisa, always felt intimidated around. She used to tease me and ask when I was going to quit dating Barbie.

"One Saturday I was waiting for my car while the oil was being changed. Across from me, coffee cup in hand, hidden behind the New York Times, was a woman, who seemed very small, maybe five-two, dressed in clothes that looked like she'd slept in them or maybe had just come from a workout without taking a shower. T-shirt, yoga pants, very 'downscale.'

"Even though I couldn't see her face, there was some- thing about the way she was sitting, legs crossed in this, "lis- ten, this is who I am, adjust" sort of way. That quiet confidence just drew me to her. I hadn't even seen her face, and I liked her already.

"When she put the newspaper aside to sip her coffee, she looked over at me. She didn't speak, but just sort of half- smiled, and went right back to her paper. She wasn't trying to impress anyone or strike up a conversation; it was clear she was just enjoying her coffee and the paper.

"Something about her was so genuine and real, I was captivated. In that moment, I felt a chill go through me, like a sort of electric shock, which surprised me, because she wasn't what I'd have considered "my type." I figured, well that's a sign. I've learned to pay attention to that sign in business, and I've made a lot of money that way, but I'd never tried it in romance, which is probably why I was 33 and had never been in a romance longer than a year or so in 18 years of dating.

"So, anyway, the next time she put the newspaper aside for a second, I asked her if she'd read about anything she'd like to do later, and if so, could I join her. And if not, could we plan something for another day.

"Of course you can guess the rest: it's been two years, we're living together now, and we will be married next year. Even my sister likes her. I cannot imagine life without her, and I thank my lucky stars, or whoever's up there watching over me, for sending me that shockwave that woke me up to the perfect life partner."

✳✳✳✳

Actually, Mark has his own Knowing to thank for encouraging him to pay attention to his sensory intuition. The Unseen World, the upper half of that infinity symbol, repeatedly sends us the perfect opportunities for us to grow spiritually, emotionally, mentally, and physically. We're the ones who usually don't notice the first time, or the second, or the 17th. But when we do, as Mark did, the payoff can be profound. When you get the hang of using your Knowing to tune into and bring toward you all the richness of life you can experience, you'll Know it's true: Life is sweet indeed. Even the rough patches are teachers.

Inward Journey Exercise 1: Blindsided

Take a few moments to write at least a paragraph or two about a time in your life when you were deeply emotionally hurt, when you felt "blindsided" by someone else's behavior. Examples include a romantic partner who simply announced, "It's over, I'm leaving," or a workplace situation in which you were treated unfairly or surprised by a job elimination or layoff.

Now, write a few paragraphs about the clues you had that these bombshells were coming. If you feel that there's no way you could have seen the situation coming, that's fine. In that case, write about what behaviors in the other parties involved *would* have tipped you off. In a week, go back over your responses to see what patterns and themes emerge. Pay attention to what you feel in and around your body as you review what you wrote. Where do you feel sensations? What are they? You may be surprised to find you did have some sensory-based insights about the situation that you overlooked. Consider them symbolic short-hand for future Knowing insights.

Inward Journey Exercise 2: Engaging the Muse

Allow yourself about 15 minutes of undisturbed time. Sit quietly and close your eyes. Do not play music as the goal is to focus on your Sensory Intuition and music may distract you. Create in your mind an awareness of someone well-known with whom you'd enjoy having an in-depth conversation (either living or deceased). While keeping your eyes closed, imagine, as completely as possible, that this person has joined you in the room and is now sitting directly across from you. Scan your skin response from head to toe, noting where you feel warmth, coolness, tingling, or any other skin-out sensation. Pay attention to any fragrances, air current movements, energy shifts, or vibrational changes that occur as you imagine yourself in conversation with this person you'd like to meet. Later, recall all that you can and record it in your Knowing Journal.

Inward Journey Exercise 3: Helping Hands

This exercise involves a partner. Sit comfortably in the chair. Close your eyes. Your practice partner should stand behind you and place one hand, palm open, between your shoulder blades. Allow yourself to really tune into the hand resting on your back for a few minutes. When you feel ready, signal your partner to remove his hand and move it about six inches away from you. Now ask your partner to fold in some fingers—one, two, three, four, or all five. Now allow yourself to sense how many fingers are still extended. Repeat the exercise 10 times, having your partner write down both how many fingers he leaves extended, and what you report, so you can easily see your progress. Don't get too caught up in being right. Pay more attention to the experience of tuning in to the sense of your partner's hand so you can learn to feel the shift from an open flat hand to one with folded-in fingers. Over time, you'll see progress if you continue to practice regularly.

CHAPTER 9
GUT/BODY—BASED
INTUITION AND KNOWING

*"Scientists, in their quest of certitude and proof,
tend to reject the marvelous."*

—Jacques Cousteau

I Knew People Were Hurt

Eight-year-old Steven of Toronto Knew about a subway accident on a train that he and his mother had just missed catching. "Mom, the train crashed," he told her as they waited on the platform for the next train.

To comfort him, she said, "No, honey, there's been no crash."

But, of course, there was. Steven felt it, deep in his body. The discomfort in his tummy told him something scary had happened, and before he could consciously form the words through thinking, he'd blurted out what he Knew. Thinking takes work, and time. But Knowing is just there, as it often is for Steven.

"It's like I just Know stuff nobody told me. It scares me sometimes," Steven said.

His mother, too, worries about what to do with Steven's sense of Knowing. "People call it a 'gift,' but I know it's a burden to him, too. I want to help him adjust to it, and use it wisely, but I'm not sure what to do," she said.

Although each person is unique, which means that exactly how each person's gut, or Gut/Body-Based Intuition, operates differs, most people find their Gut/Body-Based Intuition occurs in one (or more) of these four ways:

1. Discomfort or pain in the intestinal tract (belly or "gut," including upper and lower intestine) that is not explained by diet or disease.

2. Discomfort or pain in the neck and upper shoulders that is not explained by a medical condition.

3. A fluttering or tense feeling in the heart area, sometimes resembling the symptoms of an anxiety or panic attack, unexplained by a medical or psychological condition.

4. Sudden, sharp pain anywhere in the body that is not explained by a health problem in the person experiencing it. Later, this phantom pain is often found to represent the place on the physical body where injury occurred to someone else, almost as if the person experiencing the intuitive signal was "mirroring" it.

Over time, and with guidance, Steven will learn to deliberately access and control his Gut/Body-Based intuitive Knowing, and not fear it. Managing his gift through understanding his Intuitive Style will make his Knowing more comfortable, and both Steven and his mother happier.

Children And Gut/Body-Based Knowing

It's been said many times, and it's absolutely true: children are highly intuitive. They Know things, and haven't developed the filters to edit themselves from sharing whatever they sense. Often, as the example of Steven shows, children pick up Gut/Body-Based Intuition quite easily. This often prompts them to "blurt out" whatever they're feeling; in many ways such highly sensitive children are like children with ADD who can't sit still. I suspect that many children, and adults, with Attention Deficit Disorder may have a strong element of Gut/Body-Based Intuition in their makeup. Part of their inability to focus is that they're flooded with "data" that they don't know how to process sequentially or systematically. By encouraging the use of the Intuitive Style Profile and the techniques in this book, you might find that you can reduce some of the struggle of those you know who live with ADD.

Fear, Anxiety, and How to Tell the Difference

Fear and anxiety cloud your intuitive sense, especially your Gut/Body-based Intuition. The better you inform yourself about the real possibilities of danger, the more likely you are to relax about what's really a risk, and obtain more reliable insights that can assist you in your life. Here are a few simple things you can do right now, today, to reduce your anxiety and open the way to deeper, more reliable Knowing.

First, cut out fear-based news reports that focus on danger, destruction, and death. Your mind prefers healthy, nutritious offerings. Second, reduce your intake of violent or frightening imagery in fictional accounts such as movies, television programs, music, and video games. You'll be much calmer, because you aren't wasting adrenaline on events that initiate the hard-wired, fight-or-flight response.

At a scary movie, for example, your body reacts exactly as if the events were "real." A well-made movie that's truly frightening primes your imagination. The experience is real to your right brain, where intuition resides. In fact, if I ask you to imagine the sour taste of a lemon right now, and you really get into that experience, you'll find that your saliva glands respond *even without the lemon.* That's the power of your imagination at work. So, imagined fear creates real responses, too, as does imagined joy.

By remembering that you only have this moment, Now, and deliberately choosing how to spend it—in worry or in joy—you can significantly reduce your anxiety levels. True fear leads to the fight-or-flight adrenaline rush that happens only Now. Recall the time in your life when you were most terrified for your own survival, or a scary movie that made you scream. That's the type of adrenaline rush that true fear (or its film cousin) will produce. The rest is anxiety. As 19th-century author and humorist Mark Twain remarked, "I have known a great many troubles, but most of them never happened."

Gut or Body-Based Intuition is also commonly felt precognitively when many people die together tragically, and it is often dismissed by the experiencer. The power of numbers makes tragedies such as earthquakes, fires, floods, and airplane crashes stronger vibes, just as the sound of many violins in an orchestra is heard more powerfully than a solo one. For this reason, many people who are naturally intuitive first experience precognition, which usually centers on situations involving *others*, not themselves, and is often felt days, weeks, or months out. Although these situations may not be in our power to change, the advance awareness some people receive allows them to adjust emotionally and spiritually, releasing them from the initial shock so they may send healing, uplifting thoughts to those affected when a tragedy occurs. Many people dismiss the symptoms of their Gut/Body-Based Intuition, letting their judgments and logical left brain override the wisdom of their own body's Knowing.

To get a sense of whether Gut/Body-Based Intuition is a form upon which you rely regularly, take the following short assessment.

How to Take the Gut/Body-Based Intuition Appraisal

Read each item and circle or highlight the number that seems closest to the truth for you.

* ✳ **Circle 1** if this statement does not apply to you.
* ✳ **Circle 2** if this statement applies once in a while, but not usually.
* ✳ **Circle 3** if this statement applies sometimes.
* ✳ **Circle 4** if this statement applies pretty regularly.
* ✳ **Circle 5** if this statement applies often.
* ✳ **Circle 6** if this statement applies most of the time.
* ✳ **Circle 7** if the statement applies all the time—or almost.

| Gut/Body-Based Intuition Appraisal |

1. Even though I don't always show it,
   I feel things deeply.   1 2 3 4 5 6 7

2. I can't watch violent movie scenes
   without a strong physical reaction.   1 2 3 4 5 6 7

3. People say I have good instincts about things.   1 2 3 4 5 6 7

4. I make better "quick decisions" than most people. 1 2 3 4 5 6 7

5. I have always liked being physically active.   1 2 3 4 5 6 7

6. I become airsick or carsick easily.   1 2 3 4 5 6 7

Total, Body-Based Intuition Appraisal: _____

Now add up your scores for each section. The lowest possible score is 6, the highest is 42. Double-check your addition before recording your scores in your Knowing Journal and on the Intuitive Style Profile found on page 195.

Discerning Gut/Body-Based Intuition From Anxiety

To determine whether you're dealing with real fear or self-produced anxiety, ask yourself some questions:

1. Is this a persistent sense I have over time? A true fight-or-flight, fear-for-your-life signal is brief and prompts you into action, often before you can think about it. An example is driving uphill and suddenly pulling over just as you crest the hill, only to find a stalled car or another impediment that would have caused an accident.

2. Do I continue to get information in my dreams about this situation? If your dream life is affected, it's probably anxiety, along with your subconscious mind's attempts to bring the issue to the surface. As are most people, you may be

so busy mentally throughout the day that you the only time your subconscious can speak to you is when you are asleep, through your dreams. Developing and following a practice of meditation will reduce this response and make your body's signals easier to interpret. (Ways to fit a meditation practice into your busy life are found in Appendix D on page 205.)

3. Is this focused in the moment, in the past, or in the future? Fear-based, fight-or-flight intuition is always based in the moment, Now. You respond to the signal without thinking, without involving your logical left brain.

Many people have a difficult time differentiating between true fear and anxiety. Let me help you sort this out. If I were to ask you to think about something, you'd have to start the engine in your mind. You'd have to "put on your thinking cap," as my grandmother used to say. You'd ponder, mull over, or concentrate on the task at hand. Thinking requires a deliberate application of your conscious mind.

In the same way that inspiration often strikes in a flash after someone has spent much time developing an understanding of a subject, so too does your intuition strike in a flash to save you from danger. There is no time to think, only react. So, the better you understand your body and its cues, the more calmly and purposefully you'll react in a truly dangerous situation.

Worry and anxiety are very different from fear, in the same way that thinking is very different from intuition. Worry and anxiety are choices, which require conscious focus and deliberate effort, such as thinking. Worry takes time, as does thinking, and focuses on the future. True fear however, which is actually a form of Knowing, operates only in the present moment, Now. As de Becker notes in *The Gift of Fear* (Little, Brown, 1997), "*Worry is the fear we manufacture—it is not authentic.*"

Inward Journey Exercises

The following Inward Journey exercises are designed to help you further develop a trusted, reliable gut/body-based intuitive awareness. Choose those that seem to call to you to work with.

Inward Journey Exercise 1:
Why Worry?

To help you understand what your "worry patterns" look like, and to understand what secondary gain or hidden benefits (such as feeling like a better parent or avoiding a decision) your worries may bring you, choose a topic you're currently concerned about, and consider the following questions:

1. Am I using worry about this topic to avoid change? If you're busy worrying, often you can hang onto the status quo because you "freeze in fear" and take no action that would produce change.

2. Am I using worry about this topic to avoid admitting I can do nothing about this situation? When we feel powerless, our minds want to jump into action and find a solution. Often, that solution-finding process produces a byproduct: anxiety and worry.

3. Am I using worry about this situation as a substitute for love? The bigger question here is, do you believe that how much concern you show for someone through worry equates with how much you love him or her?

4. Am I using worry to "practice" being disappointed? Many people feel that worrying about an issue allows them to anticipate disappointment or failure, thus preparing them for it. You'd be far more relaxed and in touch with your Gut/Body-Based Intuition if you simply waited for the outcome, and reacted naturally to that, in the moment. Again, doing your best to pay attention to this moment, Now, is always your best strategy. You'll find your life is far less anxiety-ridden as a result.

5. Am I making a clear and logical assessment of the actual probability of a negative outcome? This is definitely a time to turn on your left brain. Learn the actual probabilities of various events, and you may find your anxiety is significantly reduced. For example, you are much more at risk of injury or death driving in your own neighborhood than flying on a commercial airline. Still, as many people do, you may have what is truly—at least based on probability—

an irrational fear of flying. Instead of being afraid of flying, you may be reacting to the surrender of the controls to a pilot you don't know. When driving, we feel as if we have more power, and that perceived sense of control calms us. Developing more control over those aspects of your environment which can control, such as becoming aware of your body and its signals, will allow you to worry less and to trust your Knowing more.

Inward Journey Exercise 2:
Just One Thing

Both future-oriented and past-oriented anxieties can be reduced by learning to bring yourself back to the ever present moment Now. When faced with an overwhelming array of tasks and little time, calm yourself by saying, even aloud, "I can do one thing at this moment, what will it be?" Let the rest go until that one thing is completed. This is a form of what Buddhists call mindfulness because you are focusing solely on what is right before you.

This exercise is difficult in an era that elevates multitasking to an art form. Yet we know from experience that talking on cell phones, eating, faxing, using a computer, watching a video, attending to children, changing a radio station, reading, applying makeup, or shaving while driving is dangerous (just check your auto insurance rates these past few years). And every one of us probably has done one, or more, of these attention-diverting tasks while driving, probably within the last few weeks.

Inward Journey Exercise 3:
Body Wisdom

Reflect on a situation from your own life when you were hurt emotionally or physically. You will probably discover through investigation that you had Gut/Body-Based Intuition or other signs that something was wrong. Perhaps you were one of those kids who always had a tummy ache that kept you from school. Perhaps your own child responds this way. Dig a little deeper: That gut sense is trying to protect your child, just as it tried to protect you. Perhaps there's a bully at school, or a teacher or other adult whose behavior is antagonistic or abusive in some way. Follow up on that Gut/Body-Based Intuition. Remember that it is always right in that it wants to help you.

Even when the situation doesn't allow for aversive actions, as in the case of children, who are powerless to change the choices of adults around them, Knowing is there. Often, intuition sends support. I suspect this is why more children than adults report encounters with angels. We view them as guardians and protectors, particularly in circumstances in which adults are unreliable. Your sense of Knowing may be difficult to interpret at first, but over time you'll develop a solid working knowledge of your intuitive style.

Keep a record of your body's messages for three weeks. Note each day when you awake whether and where you feel any stress, tension, or pain. Repeat the process just before you go to sleep. Watch what, if any, patterns emerge. Be sure to make notes about what emotional or spiritual issues you're facing, and see if they "resonate" to your body's signals in any way.

Although it might seem unwise to focus on the "negative" by understanding what your body is trying to tell you—and it's often about emotional and spiritual issues, not physical ones—an ongoing record is a means of decoding the signals. Over time, your body won't need to experience discomfort to send you a message about your emotional or spiritual balance; you'll learn to interpret the message without the body cues. Of course, check regularly with your healthcare professionals to ensure you're not missing something important regarding your physical health, and use relevant notes from your Knowing Journal to keep your physician informed.

Chapter 16
Gut/Body–Based
Intuition in Action

"If facts are the seeds that later produce knowledge and wisdom, then the emotions and the impressions of the senses are the fertile soil in which the seeds must grow."

—Rachel Carson

The roots of Gut/Body-Based Intuition stretch quite far back. Our ancient ancestors relied on their "gut sense" or "gut instinct" to protect them and those they cared about from danger; we still call it "mother's intuition" (fathers get it, too) when it helps us assist a child in danger. Athough the need for fight-or-flight responses is reduced in our modern times, our bodies are still "hard wired" with that deep survival instinct.

With focus and discipline you'll be able to sort the apparently random body-based intuitive signals you now receive into useful data, whether for your safety, health, and well-being or that of others. The larger goal of Knowing is to use your intuitive style in all its forms to access guiding insight to improve your life through better informed choices. To do that, you need to learn to read the clues of your Gut/Body-Based Intuition, which takes a bit of clean-up work first.

Releasing Old Patterns
of Gut/Body-Based Response

Release work is a necessary part of accessing your Body-Based Intuition in a comfortable, reliable way. While you were busy surviving all that the world has tossed at you over the several decades of your life, you've learned shortcut patterns of physical response. Even if they weren't horrible, you've had lots of adventures along the way and pulled in "stuff" from watching all those news reports. And your body has created its own responses to all that "stuff."

As a result, you sometimes "short circuit" and react as if every situation that reminds you of an old trauma is exactly the same as that first trauma. In extreme circumstances, this is called Post-Traumatic Stress Disorder, which can be treated quite successfully by trained mental health professionals. Many people also find bodywork such as massage and healing treatments helpful in releasing trauma.

If you were ever in a minor car accident and find yourself responding as if you were about to be hit again every time you drove through the area where the accident happened, you know the feeling. Other examples include soldiers who react to loud noises as if bombs, bullets, and shells are still flying around them, even months or years later. The body remembers.

Feel It to Heal It

That's why release work requires going back to and actually feeling—not reliving, but fully feeling—the original stressor. For example, when I was just 6 years old, I was accidentally electrocuted. Funny as it sounds, I didn't "feel" that experience fully enough to process it, integrate it, and release it—the steps necessary to a complete healing—until much later.

At the age of 16, I took job as a waitress. While cleaning up one night, I unplugged a counter appliance while holding a damp rag in my hand. A spark from the wall outlet sent a very small shock through me. I had what can only be called an overreaction. Basically, a meltdown. All the fears, all the sense of threat to my physical body, all the "stuff" I'd not allowed myself to feel came rushing back in that quick moment. I was a sobbing wreck for about 15 minutes, too shaky even to feel safe driving home. Embarrassed, I blamed it on fatigue and nerves. That initial release of long-held emotion was followed by several more, two of which stand out as "biggies." Face it, or face it again is the lesson I've learned.

Just after college, I lived in an apartment about 100 feet above Lake Erie and 30 feet from its shores. Watching small bits of "lightning" *in my apartment* from the highly-charged atmosphere (the result of lightening striking the lake and electrifying it) prompted me to call a fellow from my martial arts class, an electrical engineer, who screamed, "Get off the phone, now, and get to the basement!" Very wise advice, as anyone who's read the tale of lightning strike survivor Dannion Brinkley knows: never talk on the telephone during a thunderstorm.

About 10 years later, I lived two miles from Lake Erie, a good drive east of that first apartment. We had large, majestic trees in the backyard. One stormy night at about 3 a.m. the room filled with brilliant white light, accompanied by the loudest crash I've ever heard. One of our trees had been struck, causing it to shred its bark and sending its shattered limbs flying in all directions, as far as 200 feet away. I was fascinated and also saddened by the loss of that tree, part of which survived for a few more years.

I saved the oddly textured wet bark. There were sheets of it, some as long as 15 feet. I dried it in the garage and gave it to an artist friend for her weaving and assemblage projects. Other friends took pieces of the wood itself, some telling me that in Native American tradition, lightening-struck wood is considered sacred. I carried a piece of wood from that tree, about 16 inches long and 3 inches thick, around with me for a few months. The lightning strike left it with an electrical charge that persisted for a very long time. (The branch also smelled like wet, rancid bread dough for about a month, so not everyone appreciated my treasure.)

I was recovering from whiplash injuries at that time, and making a long commute to the university four days a week. I placed what I came to call my lightning stick along my spine while I drove, just because it felt good, like a pain-management unit, which also uses electrical charge to heal.

✳ ✳ ✳ ✳

After I came to appreciate the gifts the lightning strike brought me—beauty for my artist friend, sacred symbols for other friends, and healing for me—I was fully released from my fear of electricity (which of course I thought I'd dealt with decades earlier). Because I had finally integrated and processed my near-death-by-electrocution and made peace with it, I was free from the power of fear. Thankfully, I've had no more close calls with lightning, which I now find beautiful in a way I never could before, when fear kept me frozen. My Gut/Body-Based Intuition is much more reliable, too, now that fear doesn't short-circuit the process.

A controlled release and healing process to help you clear the way for your Gut/Body-Based Intuition to prosper is highly recommended over an uncontrolled release and healing process like mine. Just as you can go to the gym and exercise, but will find better results working with a trainer who guides you, you are likely to find that having a competent healing professional assist you in this healing journey makes it both more comfortable and more profound. Many professionals are trained to help you on a journey through trauma toward peacemaking and gratitude. Give yourself time. Just one example from my life took about 30 years to process; I'm still working on some others. That's part of the journey here in human form.

Reducing your fears and anxieties will also clear the clutter away so that your Gut/Body-Based Intuition can operate more reliably. Because your human body is a key element in your journey on Earth—after all, it's the only way to take a journey on Earth—developing your Body-Based Intuition is a key aspect of Knowing. The better you inform yourself about the real possibilities of danger, the more likely you are to relax about what's really a risk. The good news is that a few simple things that you can do right now, today, will help you to reduce your anxiety significantly. And even if you don't consider yourself particularly anxious, you'll be surprised at how much calmer you feel.

First, quit watching or listening to fear-based news reports which focus on danger, destruction, and death. Remember that old saying "you are what you eat"? This is true for your mind and your spirit as well as your body.

Just as your body prefers healthy, nutritious food (whatever you actually feed it), so too your mind prefers healthy, nutritious offerings. You're not only what you eat, but also what you experience. By allowing yourself to feel violent, hurtful input, you do your entire energy system a great disservice. Unless you deliberately strive to change it, what affects your subtle energy field—your aura—will eventually affect your dense energy body, the physical body you live in. Of course we can't prevent all violent, hurtful input from entering our awareness. But we *can* be selective in those areas where we do have choices, perhaps the biggest of which is our choice of entertainment. Whether it's video games, television or radio programming, movies, or books, you can choose less jarring, violent options. And that feeds your mind a steady diet of healthy input.

Ever greater numbers of studies are documenting the negative effects of violent visual content through television and video games on children. Although adults are better able to handle both real and imagined violence, why put yourself through that? Is it kind to your body, mind, and spirit? Perhaps you watch the news just to be able to chat with coworkers or others with whom you engage. If so, why? In a world of infinite possibilities, there must be something else you can discuss besides the darker side of human nature. Yes, that dark side is real. But you don't have to feed it to your thoughts and emotions. Where you put your attention shows the worlds—both the Unseen World and the Earthly World—your true intentions. And where you place your intention, you place your creative energies. You draw to you that which you focus on.

The old saying "what goes around comes around" is a folk way of interpreting that ancient law of karma. Try changing your focus for a few weeks; avoid all news programming. Keep a record in your Knowing Journal so you'll have data to assess. At the end of the experiment, see if you feel differently. My own experience is that I feel brighter, lighter, more energized, and generally much happier without introducing myself to news reports. I'm not naïve, but I'm also not a glutton for punishment. So I'm very selective about my exposure to current events.

Fear, Anxiety, and Missing the Cues of Gut/Body-Based Intuition

We routinely misunderstand fear. Generally, what we call "fear" is actually anxiety, apprehension, or worry, but Gut/Body-Based Intuition often is its messenger. When we feel Gut/Body-Based Intuition, it's typically a sign that something deep inside us is trying to come up to our waking consciousness for examination. We often misinterpret signals from Body-Based Intuition as a problem with the body itself, conveniently forgetting that body, mind, and spirit are intricately intertwined. Physicians are well aware that the majority of office visits are for things that turn out to be the result of stress or anxiety. Though they create symptoms and often are treated, the root causes are often overlooked. Our willingness to turn things over to experts and authority figures, such as physicians, attorneys, psychologists, priests, rabbis and other clergy, and trainers and coaches, does us a disservice. To first go within for some insights, to tap the inner wisdom of our own Knowing as a resource, would provide much better results when we do follow up with experts.

In my own life, I've "diagnosed" health problems by sitting with my Knowing and also paying attention to what I've observed in the Earthly World by noting patterns I'd seen in others, in my family medical history, and so on. This then led me to research, print, and take with me data for my physician to assess. She ordered tests based on this approach that led to the discovery and later resolution of some long-standing health concerns. (Later she appologized for not seeing it sooner.)

We often create reasons to worry; anxiety is a choice we make to allow ourselves to be drawn away from the Now by focusing on what might be. And again, the only place we ever have power is Now.

Perhaps you've heard the phrase "it's not what you're eating, it's what's eating you." That's a perfect example: some unacknowledged feeling is gnawing at you. Instead of sitting down to ascertain what's really going on in the moment, which requires a willingness to delve into the emotional and spiritual aspects of your life as well as the physical, as do many people, you might just head for the ice cream, cookies, or chips when you're actually lonely, sad, or angry. It's easier to have a relationship with food to salve that inner pain than to acknowledge the need for change in your life.

"Divorce would be tougher than carrying 30 or 40 extra pounds," as one client explained it to me. It was easier for her to live with the excess weight than face her fears. Over time, her Gut/Body-Based Intuition that her marriage was harmful to her spirit led her on a journey through poor health and eventually lupus, at which time her husband left her. Had she considered divorce when her Body-Based Intuition first started nagging her, she might not have had such a struggle with her health and wellness, which thankfully is back in balance. (I've noticed that autoimmune disorders such as lupus, chronic fatigue syndrome, and a wide range of other systemic or "all over" disorders appear to be a common response to a stifled Spirit.)

Knowing is gentle, persistent, and hard to miss, if you're paying attention. If you're not, your Knowing will continue to nudge you along in bigger and more varied ways, until it's essentially undeniable. That's why if you have a months—or years—of repeated dreams of your child in an accident, for example, it may be anxiety, which tends to continually bring the same message in the same way. Anxiety should always be explored, because it contains insights about your relationship with your child and will give you clues about what you might be able to change for the better within the relationship. Learning to interpret the cues your body gives you is the key, and that requires being able to tell what's fear and what's anxiety.

Precognition, Fear, and Gut/Body-Based Intuition

Being "wrong" in what seem to be precognitive insights is not "bad." Precognition, or Knowing before an event, is often considered "negative." That's because tends to happen to many people who would not otherwise consider themselves intuitive or psychic. Usually premonition involves death, injury, or destruction, and sometimes pregnancy. Why? These are the biggest possible events that can happen to us as humans. We celebrate births and honor passings with rituals; this is Big Stuff in the Earthly World.

We naturally "tune into" these events, which generally involve people quite close to us, most easily. Intuitively tuning into pending tragedies such as the 9/11 disaster, earthquakes, and other events is unusual for most people but often reported by those with a strong degree of natural-born intuition.

With practice, you will extend your ability to Know and discover that you can pick up information about all sorts of events that impact your life. In fact, you already have been receiving data, but simply couldn't interpret the signs. The entire Inward Journey toward Knowing is based on developing your personalized spiritual shorthand, of learning to read the clues in your own way.

As an example, a client of mine, whom I'll call Marilyn, had for years seen images of her son, Andrew, dying at about age 30. She often dreamt about this, but more often felt a Body-Based Intuition while awake. She'd watch him play and feel what she termed a sense of "dread" overtake her, settling around her heart. (This also is a common symptom of anxiety and panic attacks.)

Marilyn decided she was simply an overprotective, anxious mother—this was her first child, after all. These persistent images started when Andrew was just 7 years old, about six years before Andrew began using drugs. He struggled for more than 15 years with drug addictions before he died of an accidental overdose at age 29, shortly after leaving his ninth stay in a drug rehabilitation center. With the support of psychotherapy, Marilyn realizes that she is in no way responsible for her son's free will choices, which led to his addiction.

Remember that persistence is an important quality of Knowing, of inner wisdom. Her "dread" came upon her periodically, but persistently, for more than 20 years in many ways. In reflection in the years since her son died, Marilyn saw that Andrew and his father, Marcus, had always had a very volatile relationship, even when Andrew was just a 7-year-old child.

Marilyn did her best to shield Andrew from his father's outbursts, which she admits Andrew "egged on" through taunts, "button-pushing" (all children know which ones work best), and unwise choices. Even though she saw the family dynamics and arranged family counseling (which helped reduce tensions somewhat), Marilyn continued to sense that Andrew would not live long. Given that he had by this time become a heroin addict and moved across the country, her logical left brain kicked in: She realized that most addicts don't live long lives. She knew his legal problems affected his ability to work and stressed him further. After he moved away, she felt even more certain he was in trouble; somehow she hoped her mother-love would turn things around for Andrew. Her body-based intuitive signals became even stronger. Over time, perhaps to manage her mounting anxiety, Marilyn prepared herself for what she saw as the inevitable: she would lose Andrew as a young man, just as she'd always felt she would. Sadly, it happened.

As most of us do at different points, the gut/body-based signals her intuition was sending Marilyn through the "dread" she felt settling around her heart were easily dismissed. Left-brain logic kicked in: *I'm being overprotective. He's my only son, my oldest. Of course people with addictions are more prone to early death.*

The changes in the wake of Andrew's death are good ones in many ways, however. Marilyn is closer than ever to Marcus, her husband of more than 40 years. She lectures widely on her experiences, hoping to spare another family the pain with which she's lived with. Most importantly, Marilyn lives with no regrets, Knowing that she always did (and still does) her best. And she definitely encourages people to heed the gut/body-based cues they receive.

Judgment, Knowing, and Your Dark Side

Please do not judge yourself if you've missed those gut/body-based intuitive cues during your life; we all have. Judgment and an overly critical stance shut down your Knowing. Making errors is how we learn, how we gain knowledge in this end of the infinity loop, the Earthly World. The "dark side" of human nature, what I prefer to view as unenlightened, free-will choice, certainly exists. But you can take greater control of your own life, through your own Knowing, by making it a practice to assess the darker side of *your* human nature.

Only by delving into those dark places—and we all have them—can we learn to release the negativity, the pain, and the fear operating in those musty basement corners of our psyches. Bring your dark aspects up from the messy basement of your subconscious mind into the light of your own Knowing, where the power your Knowing Self will lead you to make better choices. As a result, you will learn how to live more fully, more freely, more richly, more gratefully—from the awakened inner wisdom of Knowing.

Chapter 11
Mixed Intuition and Knowing

"There are only two ways to live your life. One is as though nothing is a miracle. The other is as though everything is."

—Albert Einstein (1879-1955)

I Kept Seeing Signs

Mark, a 33-year-old marketing manager in the Boston area, had wanted to open his own market research consultancy for a few years. With 10 years' experience, an MBA degree, and a background in applied statistics, he had the requisite credentials, and even a few possibilities for partners as well as some potential clients. But in a tough economy, and with plans for a family with his wife of four years, Amy, the timing seemed all wrong. Mark decided he'd consider reaching for his dream again in seven to 10 years. But his timetable changed, because of the repeated signs he began to receive.

"I'm what you'd call a true skeptic; left-brained all the way. Show me the data. So I was surprised when I kept seeing, feeling, and hearing signs that seemed to be from my dad's dad, who died of a heart attack a few months after we

got married. Every way I could get a sign encouraging me to pursue my dream, I received one. They were everywhere. Awake, asleep, I got signs. I'd think, Nah, can't be, and then I'd get three more signs in the next three days. It got to be pretty funny," Mark explained.

"I'd be driving to work, and I'd see a reference to my childhood nickname, Climber Monkey (that my grand-father, called me), on the back of a truck in front of me. There it'd be, some reference to monkeys, or climbing. Once I saw references to both those terms on the same 20-minute drive," Mark recalled.

"A few days after that one, I was out on calls for work. I pulled up to a red light, and noticed the address of the corner I was stopped at was my granddad's birth-day, which was March 12, 1935. There I was at 31235! I consider it a sign from him."

"Amy said, 'Just go with it, see where it leads' but I just am not that way. I'm very logical. I decided to test it out. I figured that if I continued to get these random signs, when I had at least, oh, 20 or so, I'd start to believe maybe something's up. So I tracked it.

"Within a five-week period, I had 27 signs involving my childhood nickname, Climber Monkey; the teenage variation, Monk (which wasn't funny since I went to a Catholic school) the fishing boat he used to have, which he named Ellie Girl after my grandmother, Eleanor; the street he lived on, Treeline Drive; and songs on the ra-dio, too. Even a news report brought me a little message. Piecing it all together was like solving a puzzle. I started getting into it, wondering, What message will I get to-day?

"I began having dreams with my granddad, where we were sitting in Ellie Girl, on a lake, as we used to when I was a kid, talking about my life, especially the business. I was wondering if I was losing it.

"I'm a logical guy, but here I am, having these vivid dream visits, which felt like real encounters, with my grandfather long after he's died. And he's saying, 'You know you want to do this, why not give it a try? I'll help you. Let me help you.'

"I am so hard to convince. I'm thinking, starting a business is what I want to do, so of course I'm going to dream about it and notice signs that confirm what I want to do," Mark said. *"And that's when it really got strange. I was sitting on the back deck with my laptop, checking e-mail, late one Friday afternoon when the screen suddenly changed to a picture—I swear I am not making this up—of, you guessed it, a climber monkey. And I am sure I heard my granddad laughing, too,"* Mark said, smiling at the memory.

"The hair stood up on the back of my neck, I felt very alert and sort of nervous. It was so unexpected and just odd. I remember thinking, Okay, you finally got my attention. I don't know how he did it, or if he did it, but I figured, that's enough, because I was starting to get a little spooked. Next time he might just walk into the room while I'm having dinner. So I decided, why not investigate the possibilities, really see if this business is viable. If it's not, I'll look at it again some other time, as I'd planned anyway. But it's been two years now, and the business is going better than I could have dreamed. I consider my granddad my most reliable silent— well maybe not silent—partner. I still get signs from him," Mark added.

✳✳✳✳

As Mark did, you may be someone who receives signs through Mixed Intuition. Find out your level of Mixed Intuition as you build your Intuitive Style Profile by taking the following Mixed Intuition Appraisal.

How to Take the
Mixed Intuition Appraisal

Read each item and circle or highlight the number that seems closest to the truth for you.

* ✳ **Circle 1** if this statement does not apply to you.
* ✳ **Circle 2** if this statement applies once in a while, but not usually.
* ✳ **Circle 3** if this statement applies sometimes.
* ✳ **Circle 4** if this statement applies pretty regularly.
* ✳ **Circle 5** if this statement applies often.
* ✳ **Circle 6** if this statement applies most of the time.
* ✳ **Circle 7** if the statement applies all the time—or almost.

Mixed Intuition Appraisal

1. I can do or think about several things at the same time pretty easily.   1 2 3 4 5 6 7

2. I'm a creative, "out-of-the-box" thinker, or am often told I am.   1 2 3 4 5 6 7

3. When I'm in a social setting, I can follow several conversations at the same time pretty easily.   1 2 3 4 5 6 7

4. I'm easily distracted by sights, sounds and movements around me.   1 2 3 4 5 6 7

5. I need lots of variety in my work or I get bored.   1 2 3 4 5 6 7

6. I have a hard time staying mentally focused on the same thing for too long.   1 2 3 4 5 6 7

Total, Mixed Intuition Appraisal: _____

Now add up your scores for each statement. The lowest possible score is 6, the highest is 42. Double-check your addition before recording your scores in your Knowing Journal and on the Intuitive Style Profile found on page 195. Your Mixed Intuition Appraisal score will have greater meaning as you complete the Intuitive Style Profile.

If you want to just move quickly through the Intuitive Style Profile sections and return later to the development exercises for each type, see page 39 (Visual Intuition Appraisal), page 60 (Auditory Intuition Appraisal), page 80 (Sensory Intuition Appraisal), and page 98 (Body-Based Intuition Appraisal).

Feel free to jump ahead to page 131 to complete the first part of your Intuitive Style Profile; you now have appraisal scores from the five major types of intuition with which to work. But the observational data from practicing with your Knowing in real-world settings is extremely valuable, too, so make time for a few of the following exercises.

Mixed Intuition Inward Journey Exercises

To sharpen your Mixed (or Mulisensory) Intuition, choose a few of the following exercises. Let your intuition guide you to the ones that seem right for you at this time. Be sure to take notes of your experimentation process in your Knowing Journal; you'll use the themes and patterns that emerge as part of the experiment in discovery of your own intuitive style, your way of Knowing.

Inward Journey Exercise 1: Noticing Repetitive Signs

These signs are likely to be subtle, and to appear on a variety of sensory triggers. For example, you may wonder what step to take next in your marriage, and see a bakery delivery truck with a wedding cake and white doves as you drive to work. The next day, you might notice doves in your yard. The third day, you might hear songs on the radio that were played at your wedding. And the fourth day, you might feel the energetic presence of your grandmother, whose anniversary it happens to be, although she'd died a decade earlier. All these signs together might encourage you to work harder at your marriage, based on the mixed, but repeated, intuitive signals you received.

Just as a scientist keeps a log of his experiments to learn what works and what doesn't, as an explorer of your own consciousness, you'll discover that logging your progress guides you toward what works and away from what doesn't for your *own* Knowing, which is unlike anyone else's (so comparing notes won't help much, although it's fun).

Create a template to organize the information. You'll find an example of how to set one up in Appendix B on page 200. Once you have at least a few weeks' worth of observational data, you're ready to work with the material to see what patterns emerge. You can also use highlighter markers or colored pencils to sort out what the links and associations are. If you prefer, organize your data on index cards, or in a database or spreadsheet program on your computer so you can sort it by keywords to discover more than one pattern.

In the example shown in Appendix B, many of the signs were related to birds. That would suggest a need to explore what birds mean, and what that might represent. Example: *Am I being "flighty?" Am I trying to fly away from my problems? Am I not eating well, eating "like a bird" when I need more nutrition?* And so on.

You may find it helpful to conduct this exercise during the same time frame as a few friends conduct it. Then, you can share your data and let them suggest patterns and associations that you may not have seen. Even if you work with friends, always let your own inner wisdom, your own Knowing, guide you as you assess the patterns and trends in the data you receive as you interact with the Earthly World and the Unseen World. Only you can say what the meaning of your life is. By paying attention, and keeping a record, you'll soon see how interconnected the two worlds are.

Inward Journey Exercise 2:
Total Body Check-In

Allow 10 to 15 minutes of quiet time for this exercise, which guides you through the process of "checking in" with your primary senses so that you learn to solicit feedback from all of them. After all, they all report data to you. As a scientific observer of your own Knowing, it's to your benefit to access and review all the data available.

Sit or lie down comfortably, so that your body is balanced symmetrically. Close your eyes gently. Do not play music, for your goal is to attend only to what your body brings you in this moment. Have a pen and paper or a recording device nearby so that you can document the exercise. As you breathe in slowly and regularly, pay close attention to how your body feels with each breath. Notice how inhaling fills your lungs and expands your abdomen, and how exhaling feels. After a few relaxing, slow breaths, check in with your visual sense notice what images appear on the "screen" of the inside of your closed eyes. If you see nothing, that's fine; make a mental note to record later that you only saw the inside of your eyelids. If you see patterns, colors, or images that prompt associations, notice and mentally record (or use equipment to record) those associations. Each time you're prompted to an association, remind yourself to come back to the sensory input your body is receiving in the moment, Now. You may find that your mind wanders often; that's fine. Just bring it back to the moment, Now.

Next, notice what sounds you hear. Distant sounds, close sounds, the sound of your steady breathing, the sound of your heartbeat, the sound of your blood pulsing—mentally note all of it.

Now turn to your Sensory Intuition, the "field" energy around you. What is the atmosphere in this moment? What is the temperature of the room or the environment? Where is heat, light, or coolness striking you? How does your skin feel? What is your skin telling you at this moment? Where do you feel discomfort—itchiness, twitchiness, changes of temperature? Scan your skin from your scalp to the soles of your feet and just notice what you experience.

Next, turn your attention inward. Focus on your stomach, your intestines, and all the other inner organs you generally don't think about but that serve you so well each day. Note where you feel discomfort, heaviness, fullness, or any other sensation; if you can't find words for it, remember how it feels so you can document it later.

Now, allow yourself to just be for a moment, to fully experience the moment, Now. No thinking, no assessing, nothing but Being.

When you feel ready to open your eyes, do so gently. Write down or record your experiences. Notice which of the different areas of your awareness (Visual, Auditory, Sensory, or Gut/Body-Based) was the easiest to access, and which was the most difficult. Where did you find your mind wandering the most? Were there any points at which you felt more than one sensory experience vying for your attention? All of your responses are important data for the experiment in developing your own Knowing.

Take care not to go from this exercise into a situation where you are required to focus intently, such as driving. Allow yourself a period of adjustment.

Inward Journey Exercise 3:
Soul Music

Just as certain music will strike you in a particular place in your body, so too will what I call the "soul music" of others.

You can easily do this exercise for a few minutes or for as long as you like, so it's a good one to keep in mind for times when you're waiting. Find a busy place such as an airport, a shopping mall, a busy park, a sporting event, or another area where you can observe people easily from a distance of about 10 to 20 feet. Have something handy to take notes, or record vocally (although this may be difficult to do in a public setting).

Your goal is not to conduct a "reading" or gather information about the life circumstances or character of the passersby; your goal is simply to notice how your instrument, your body, responds to the vibrations and frequencies—the soul music—of others.

As people pass by, sense the energy they are generating, the music they're playing (we all do it, consciously or not; consciously is better). Pay attention to which form of your intuition is most activated by different people. Do you get a strong visual response to some people? A more gentle sensory response at your skin or just beyond it with others? Do some "speak" to you in your mind's ear? Are others simply "blank" to you? Document your responses, and notice any patterns that emerge. Do you find it easiest to tune into children? People about your own age? Men or women? Do people who seem agitated cause more difficulty for you than calmer, gentler sorts, or are they easier to tune into? Do people who resemble your parents, family members, or workplace colleagues cause any anxieties or concerns that shut down your Knowing? Do you find yourself awash in responses on several levels—Visual, Auditory, Sensory, or Gut/Body-Based? It's all data for the experiment in your Knowing, so take good notes about your experiences.

As you assess the information, notice any patterns that emerge and highlight that information. You may be quite surprised at what you discover about yourself.

Power Points Exercises

These short exercises are designed to support you as you practice with your Knowing to sort out your particular Intuitive Style Profile; they're meant to be used whenever you think to do so, ideally several times a day.

Power Points Exercse 1:
Small Graces

As you move through your day, extend yourself outward to others in small ways. This way you present intention in action, which serves your higher purpose as well as being in service to others. You don't have to let anyone know you are doing these little gestures on their behalf, and be sure to include both people you know and those you've never met.

Power Points Exercise 2:
Take a Bow

Think of a favorite song. Close your eyes and create it in your mind. Allow yourself to see, hear, and feel—both outside and inside your body—how this song affects you. Now, imagine yourself on a stage in a large arena, singing beautifully (don't worry if you can't sing; this is an exercise in intention) to a huge crowd of adoring fans. Get clear images of your band, your backup singers, dancers, and lighting. Add whatever makes your imaginary concert as powerful and real as possible. You are sharing the gift of your special music, the song of your soul, of your spirit, with the audience. Remember that you have a unique and special voice and that only you can share this gift with the audience, the rest of the Earthly World. Take a bow. And whenever you need a quick reminder of how special you are, face a mirror and take a bow as a reminder of your uniqueness and to honor your special self.

Seeds of Success: The Power of Intention

Awareness of our intentions makes life much more focused and rewarding. What you intend resonates in the world, harmonizing with like vibrations and resonances. So, if your intention is to develop a strong, reliable Mixed Intuition then choose from the following suggested affirmations. This is the last stop on the train, it all ends up here with whichever "line" with which you begin: Visual, Auditory, Sensory, or Gut/Body-Based. Better yet, create your own with words that resonate to your personal Knowing. Be sure to keep your affirmations in the Now by phrasing them in the present tense; use "I am" not "I will be."

* ✳ "My intuitive Knowing supplies me many types of signs, gently and persistently encouraging my understanding."

* ✳ "I clearly sense and deeply Know what is best for me and I act on it, carefully and wisely."

* ✳ "My Mixed Intuition is like a circle of friends who love me and offer me guidance."

CHAPTER 12
MIXED INTUITION
IN ACTION

"Science is organized knowledge. Wisdom is organized life."

—Immanuel Kant

Just as your body is a holistic, interconnected system, so is your intuitive style, the culminating form of the intuitive style that, along with your values, comprises the foundation of your Knowing. In many ways, Mixed Intuition is the merging and blending of the other four types of intuition. Mixed Intuition also is a catch all category for those guiding signs and messages that are not easily interpreted as primarily Visual, Auditory, Sensory, or Gut/Body-Based. Many people operate primarily from Mixed Intuition. It both transcends and includes the other intuitive styles. Although it stands on its own as a distinct intuitive style, it also represents the most mature, evolved form of Sensory Intuition.

Mixed Intuition signs tend to arrive on several levels at once and are more commonly experienced by people who have made intuitive development, spiritual practice, or meditation a part of their lifestyles. Essentially, Knowing is learning to interpret the language of your own soul. And like learning a language carving out time and opportunities to practice will increase your fluency in interpreting the symbolism of your intuitive signs and building a reliable shorthand symbol system.

Here are the different ways Mixed Intuition operates:

Sequential Mixed Intuition: This is when a person receives a series of intuitive or symbolic signs, as Mark did. They tend to "cluster" and have the sense of what famed 20th-century psychologist Carl Jung named synchronicity, or meaningful coincidence. Often, the signs and messages include both outward signs found in the world around the person, and inner awareness signs experienced through the senses.

Embedded Mixed Intuition: This is when a person receives intuitive signs on more than one sensory channel at once; the meanings are so tightly connected they are embedded within each other, or enmeshed. An example is an auditory intuitive sign, such as hearing a voice while also smelling a fragrance, both associated with a particular person, living or deceased. By investigating further through attention and focus, a person might understand that these signs are meant to encourage or dissuade a particular choice being considered, for example.

Literal Mixed Intuition: Signs that have literal meaning, usually found in the outside world, delivered through someone else, or via the dream state. An example is hearing a song on the radio play, such as "Money, Money, Money" just as you are on your way to the bank to complete a beneficial loan refinance. Other examples include dreaming the name of a book that contains relevant information to a current life issue, or seeing a meaningful number. Many people report noticing a digital clock with a loved one's birthday, such as 10:17 for October 17, repeatedly during certain periods of their lives.

Usually periods of repetitive signs are important choice points in people's lives, or mark times of big change. Mixed Intuition often comes at times when we most need guidance and support through our Knowing and often take the form of messages from deceased loved ones through after-death communication and mediumship. Over time, most people discover these types of signs diminish as their inner awareness and trust in their own Knowing expands. They trust their own Knowing enough at that stage of their intuitive development not to need external confirmation, although it's always nice to receive.

Mixed Intuition in Operation

Embedded signs are "packed" and, like a downloaded file for your computer that you want to execute, are zipped or compressed with many layers of meaning. You must unpack them to understand the full message. That's an advanced skill, so don't worry too much about it if you're just beginning to develop your intuition and your Knowing. When learning to read, you first learn individual letters, then you work your way up to sequential letters, build up to phonics, then to words and sentences. Sequential signs are like the letters that make up words; embedded signs are like complete sentences. The more you work with the "letters" the better you'll get at words. So initially, you're more likely to receive mixed intuitive signs sequentially.

The "whammo" feeling of being hit (energetically speaking) with a lot of information all at once is an adventure to look forward to, although a bit disconcerting at first for many people. The unmistakable feeling of, *Well, there's a message I can't ignore* is the point. It's often been said that your soul speaks to you gently at first. If not heeded, the signs become louder and more difficult to ignore. This is why being unattached to a particular outcome while having a general sense of life direction, of living with resilience and flexibility, will serve you best as you learn to expand your Knowing.

People who have a well-developed meditation practice naturally become very intuitive. Those who work to develop their intuitive skills also tend to experience these "big signs" or embedded signs experienced on several levels at once. We all are intuitive, but, as with any other talent, some people possess more natural ability.

Even for those with natural ability, discerning which channel to pay attention to first is the challenge when Mixed Intuition brings information on several channels at once. I suspect that many people who have Attention Deficit Disorder could be experiencing a form of sensory overload, rather like the embedded sign form of Mixed Intuition.

In practice, embedded signs are quite common for me when I am conducting mediumship demonstrations, in which the energy of a person who's passed on blends with my own energy field. Usually the person from the Unseen World signals me in several ways at once, embedding several meanings in one quick hit, producing a by-now-familiar energetic *whammo* feeling, a rush of energy. This energy rush is why mediums tend to speak faster than normally while presenting messages, or move around as they present information. It's a way of dissipating the overwhelming energy.

At such times I've often found myself writing a person's name backwards in the air (which makes my "writing" viewable to an onlooker facing me) with my left hand while simultaneously announcing it. Although I'm left-handed, I don't write backwards except when prompted in this way. This is an example of an embedded sign containing auditory and sensory data. Neither the hand motion nor the announcing of the name feels like something I was attempting to do; it just "blurts out." This is sometimes called an *automism* by observers. As an experiencer of the phenomenon, I call it the Ultimate Improv: you never know who's in the scene with you or where it's going to go when you trust your Knowing enough to completely go with the flow. Other times I'll find myself holding the upper right quadrant of my abdomen while mentioning that I feel the energy of a woman who died of liver cancer, an example of an embedded sign that is auditory and body-based. At other times, I'll motion to my left leg then drawing a line up to the chest and around my heart, which is my sign for someone who had an angioplasty, while also saying that. This is another example of an embedded sign that is both auditory and body-based. I have enough control now (although not as a child) about how I receive information through Knowing, that I could dispense with the hand signals if I chose to. But it's confirming as well fun for me, plus I sometimes find new ways of perceiving information, adding to my growing symbolic shorthand dictionary. It's also instructive to those watching because they, too, learn how embedded signs work. (For more about mediumship and its relationship to Knowing, see Chapter 15.)

Over time you will learn to pace the communications you receive through the embedded signs of Mixed Intuition, but beginners often feel rushed to get all the words out before they lose the information. It's like waking from a dream, which is also an altered state of consciousness; you must record the dream quickly or it will evaporate. Developing personal discipline and practicing with a group will help you balance the flow of Knowing immensely. Be sure that the group you choose to work with is not interested in "flashy" mediumship, in which stage presence, extraneous movement or fast speech is confused with good mediumship. Information on practice group resources can be found on page 217.

Visual and auditory cues are also commonly joined in an embedded sign. I might see the cover of a particular CD, for example, in my mind's eye while mentally hearing a song that is from that CD.

Although I generally don't have knowledge of the music itself, in such a situation I work from the place of inner Knowing, trusting that the knowledge is accurate, which it usually is, unless I'm misinterpreting the cues. If I am, I'll continue to receive embedded signs until I figure it out.

Ask and You Shall Receive

Learning to access Mixed Intuition, whether via sequential signs, embedded signs, literal signs, or symbolic signs, reduces errors in interpretation. For those seeking to improve accuracy in working with intuition or mediumship, requesting these embedded signs before you begin your sessions is a good strategy.

Once a gentleman from the Other Side showed me his job, which I correctly identified as factory work in a small company in the 1950s and 1960s. But it was through the hand motions I made that his granddaughter identified him. Both of her grandfathers had been factory workers, but her paternal grandfather had been both an owner and a drill press operator in a small factory the family had once owned. She'd often seen him at work as a teenager, when she helped out after school. This is not work I know a thing about, but which had very specific hand motions she recognized that differentiated him from her other grandfather, who worked in an automobile manufacturing plant. Sometimes it's the small, repetitive signs that are the most telling evidence of guidance around us.

Mark's story of guidance from his grandfather demonstrates series of repetitive signs which come on different sensory channels. For Mark, and many people who have not worked to develop their intuition and Knowing, the "big sign" is less common. Instead of that unmistakable "whoosh" that floods the senses, the pace is slower, but the message, through repetition on a number of intuitive channels, is unmistakable.

In Sequential Mixed Intuition, the messages come via Visual Intuition, other times Auditory, Sensory, or Body-Based Intuition. This type often prompts us toward Knowing, as it did for Mark, which always involves analysis and intuition. Often, as in his case, the messages are from passed-on loved ones who are pointing toward reinforcing cues in the world around us, through images, sounds, memories, and associations that quickly remind us of them. It's that quickness that suggests that these sequential multisensory cues are actually intuition at work. Of all possibilities, why would a person remember his or her piano teacher from childhood upon seeing a hummingbird at a feeder? Lots of people you've run across in 20 or 30 or 50 or 60 years of living had hummingbird feeders. The classic question, *Why this, why now?* is an excellent one to ask under circumstances such as these.

The answer might be that the piano teacher had a hummingbird feeder which was easily viewed from the piano where lessons took place. The association was made because the person experiencing the association, the moment of intuitive insight, was considering whether to take up lessons again 30 years later. In such a case, the association is probably a sign. Because Knowing operates as a series of gentle promptings, the experience of a "sign" will probably be repeated, in a variety of ways, as it was for Mark. Taking time to make a decision is wise. If you are meant to have a particular experience, such as rediscovering music as an adult, your intuitive signs, often sequential multisensory signs, will keep pushing you toward that goal.

Always conduct a logical analysis, too: will piano lessons fit into the family budget? Is there time in your schedule? The left and right hemispheres of the brain were designed to work together to bring you your best life.

Literal Mixed Intuition is just that: quite literal. Still, meaning is often missed because we are trying to make something stand for more than it is. Sometimes, as Sigmund Freud pointed out, a cigar is just a cigar. But usually, that's not the case. On many occasions in my work, I've had very literal intuitive signs that I completely misunderstood because I presumed they must be metaphors, or symbols of something else.

In a private session with a lovely gentleman in his 70s who'd lost his beloved wife to cancer, I saw/heard/felt the Challenger explosion from 1986 on a Mixed Intuition level. I presumed it was a symbol, suggesting that losing his wife was like an explosion in his life that left him in deep grief, quite "challenged," if you will. Although that was an accurate interpretation, in this case the sign of the Challenger explosion was actually literal. It turns out the man had trained many astronauts in his 50-year career, both in military service and as an employee of a manufacturer of airplanes. Among the many astronauts he'd trained were those who died in the Challenger disaster, as well as three others who'd perished in 1967 in the launch explosion accident involving Apollo IV. Just as his wife was stopping by from the Other Side, so were his colleagues.

Should you choose to work with your intuition and your Knowing over a period of years, you too will notice that the symbolic shorthand you receive has a similar quality as my Challenger example. Like that sign, yours intuitive signs will tend to be both Literal and Symbolic, both Visual and experienced on Body-Based, Sensory, and/or Auditory levels—simultaneously.

It All Has Meaning

Among the most fascinating aspects of human consciousness is how we make associations, how we assign meaning. While certain symbols have a universal or archetypal meaning—the creation myth of gods and goddess mating to create a particular nation, a familiar folk tale theme found in all parts of the world—it's all part of that deep well of life experience and common, shared knowledge.

Gestalt psychology teaches us that there is a whole, which is comprised of a foreground and a background which ebb and flow. Certain feelings, memories, and experiences seem to come to the forefront of our attention based on the stimuli we receive. What comes to the foreground from all the available possibilities (infinite possibilities) therefore has meaning for us.

That's exactly the way to look at the repeated-message form of Mixed Intuition. What comes to the foreground? What draws your attention? Why are you "pulled" to look over to a street sign, just to see that it's your just-passed mother's name on the sign? Why does a song you associate with a particular person play on a station that ordinarily doesn't play it, exactly on the anniversary of that person's death? Why does a book with a title that addresses exactly what you're evaluating in your life fall off the shelf at the bookstore, right at your feet?

I have no answer for the "why" questions. We may never know why until we're back in the Unseen World, our true home; even then, we may not receive those particular answers. The inward journey here in the Earthly World is designed to be taken largely on faith. Faith in some higher power? Perhaps. Faith that the only way to Know our way in this world is through the instruments of our bodies, minds, and spirits? Absolutely.

While we journey individually and collectively (aren't you glad you have company for this trek?) here in the Earthly World, we can work with signs much more pragmatically, leaving philosophy and "why" questions for later. Synchronicities and magical, wonderful things do happen, and they happen consistently.

> *"Miracles, in the sense of phenomena we cannot explain, surround us on every hand:*
> *life itself is the miracle of miracles."*
>
> —*George Bernard Shaw (Preface to Androcles and the Lion)*

Instead of spending precious life energy on the how and why questions, from the place of Now (the only place you ever have authentic, true power), worry about What: What to do with this information, What it means, to me, Now. Don't compare notes with your neighbor on this test; it's yours and yours alone. Only what *you* make of it matters; not what your friend says, what your psychic tells you, or what your dream dictionary offers. While those perspectives may be insightful in leading you to new shades and textures of meaning, the meaning that *you* assign to events in your life is the meaning that matters—the *only* meaning that matters. It's *your* Knowing, after all. Yours and yours alone, your unique and special worldview.

Surrendering to the Process

I enjoy the experience of surrendering to the process of blending energy during mediumship by using Knowing and deliberately finding and using that crossing-point juncture between the Unseen World and the Earthly World, where the two loops of the infinity symbol meet (see Figure 1 on page 17).

I have ground rules, of course, for what energies I will and will not accept, and on what terms. As I am, you are always, always, always in charge of what energies you allow to merge and blend with your own energy. Through declaration of your intentions you determine the ground rules. Some people believe they need what is often called psychic protection. I suggest that you instead work from a place of positive intention and declaration. The word *protection* is negative because it injects fear into the equation, which will limit your Knowing.

Chapter 13
Putting It All Together: Your Intuitive Style Code

"Trust your own instinct. Your mistakes might as well be your own, instead of someone else's."

—Billy Wilder

At this point in the process of investigating your way of Knowing, you have information about the five basic building blocks of your natural intuitive style. In the next several chapters, we'll be adding information about values, personal symbolism, and your way with others to further develop a sense of your intuition in action. But for now, let's pull together the five basic building blocks of your Intuitive Style.

Determining Your Two-Letter Intuitive Style Code

Transfer your five appraisal scores which represent different elements of your Intuitive Style—Visual (page 39), Auditory (page 60), Sensory (page 80), Gut/Body-Based (page 98), and Mixed (page 115). Enter the numbers you scored in the boxes next to the word Score in the following chart. Then, using the numbers at the left for reference, place an X or dot directly above each score, near the line that approximates the number that you scored on each of the different appraisals of the Intuitive Style Inventory. Connect the dots to show the pattern of your intuition. Jot down the initials of your top two scores. For example, GS is the code for someone whose highest score is Gut/Body-Based and whose second highest score is Sensory; VA is the two-letter code for someone whose highest score is Visual and whose second highest score is Auditory.

42					
35					
26					
21					
14					
6					
Scale:	V	A	S	G	M
Score:					

Two-Point Intuitive Code: ____

Your Two-Point Code

Your two-point Intuitive Style Code is helpful information about your natural-born intuitive style, but please realize that it is only a guideline that provides an initial, basic awareness. Richer, more nuanced and textured meaning arises through the process of analysis. Don't worry; this won't be difficult and it won't matter if you weren't a math or statistics whiz. In fact, it's better if you don't make this more complex than necessary. With that in mind, I've kept this process deliberately simple. Basically all you have to do is pay attention to the patterns in the data, both the numeric or quantitative data, and the nonnumeric or qualitative data (you'll find most of that in your Knowing Journal). That's information that will add depth and texture to the interpretations of this more quantitative material. We'll deal with that later; for now, it's all about the patterns in the numbers.

As a researcher and investigator of your own process of Knowing, you're seeking to understand the themes and patterns which emerge from this information. Also remember that the process of developing your intuition and your Knowing is ongoing, so different aspects of your natural-born intuition will ebb and flow over time, depending on where you place your attention and your intention, your reflection, and your evolution.

These four key aspects, Intention, Attention, Reflection, and Evolution (which can be abbreviated to the four letters I A R E, an intriguing, if ungrammatical, extension of the well-known spiritually powerful phrase, I AM), are discussed in Chapter 18.

Here's a simple approach to assessing your scores.

Clustering of Scores

First look at the overall pattern of scores. Do you see a cluster of scores in the highest ranges of the chart, more than 35? Or, are your scores distributed across the mid-ranges (between 21 and 35)? Perhaps your scores are all clustered in the lower ranges of the score report (at 20 or less). People who score high tend to be more confident in their overall sensory awareness, while those who score lower tend to be less reliant on sensory input. You might say that those who score high are more in touch with their right-brain style, while those who score lower are more in touch with their left-brain style. If you find your scores tend to cluster in the lower ranges, one challenge you will face is developing confidence in your natural-born intuition. By working with the exercises you'll find throughout this book, you'll be able to develop your natural-born intuition into a more trusted, focused resource for Knowing your way in the world. Don't lose heart. High scores are not necessarily better. Remember that this self-appraisal process is designed to give you information about *you*.

Many people report a pattern of scores in which they have two scores very close together, followed by a third, which is also fairly close to the highest number. An example is 41-39-36. Keep in mind that 41 is a full five points higher than 36, about 14 percent higher. That's a pretty significant difference. As a general rule of thumb, consider scores separated by three or fewer points as close.

Ties Among Scores

Pay most attention to the highest and second-highest scores, particularly if you have a second-place tie (for example two scores of 33). In such a situation, let your intuition be your guide (you knew I'd say that somewhere didn't you?) as to which of the two scores is most comfortable and natural to you. It also helps to see where your score for Mixed Intuition falls. Very often, people with strong Mixed Intuition demonstrate patterns with ties with in the midrange scores. Again, there are no hard and fast answers. This is a process of investigation. It's dynamic and ever-changing—just like you!

Differences Between Scores
Highest-to-Lowest

Now take a look at the numeric spread among your different appraisal scores. What is the numeric difference between your highest and your lowest self-reported scores? For example, is your highest score 41and your lowest score 23? Or, perhaps your lowest score is 34. A person who reports a high-low score differential of 18 is very different in his or her Intuitive Style compared to someone whose high-low score differential is 7.

Spread of Scores
Highest to Second-Highest

Now notice the numeric differential between your highest and second-highest appraisal scores. Are they very close together? That's important data; if your two highest scores are only one or two points apart, for practical purposes, you have a tie. This means that you must be very aware of which of the two foundational elements of your intuitive style is at work in any given moment. All it takes is practice and focus; you'll get the hang of it.

There are 20 basic Intuitive Style Patterns (including auditory, body-based, sensory, and visual as the only intuition experience). Again, your distribution of scores and the patterns in the data are as important as the following "short takes" on your particular style of intuition. By working with it, and adding the quantitative data, you'll develop your intuition into that reliable, practical inner wisdom I call Knowing. This information helps ground the process, but don't get "stuck" on your two-point code. You're way more than your blood type, right? That's the way to look at this: you're far more complex than your Intuitive Style Code.

Your Intuitive Style

The results of your responses to the various intuitive appraisals that you provide today will not be the same as the answers you'll provide a year from now, or even a few months from now. As you learn to extend your senses and blend them, you'll discover the process is much more dynamic than static, much more malleable than fixed. You are likely to find that you have a few basic building blocks that serve as "old reliables." Still, you may discover that attending to your Auditory Intuition brings it on so strongly that, for a while at least, it becomes a particular favorite intuitive style.

I won't suggest that this is entirely like fashion, that you change your intuitive style each season, but in some ways working with your intuitive style is like working with your fashion sense over time. You probably have a few great colors or styles that you know work well for you, and some that just never seem to work no matter how much the magazines and your friends foist them on you. Over time you build on your basic style year after year to create your distinct and special "look" by updating your wardrobe with new pieces to reflect your changing tastes and what's popular at the moment your intuition is like that. Your Intuitive Style responds to updates and changes. You're going to make some major intuitive "faux pas," just as you probably made some definite fashion "don'ts" at some point in your life. (Remember that bridesmaid dress, or the outfit you wore on vacation that makes you cringe when you see it now in old photos?)

So, if you're seeking easy answers that fit forever, you're likely to be disappointed. Even when your personal fashion style fits well for long periods of time, just like a great hat or a handbag that you love, you might be simply become tired of it. Trends change. Your color preferences change, your body changes, your lifestyle changes even more. Think of your intuition in much the same way as your style of dress. That's why understanding your Intuitive Style as both fundamental to who you are, and also an expression of who you are, will help you get the most out of it. I promise you, the information you glean from this process will serve you throughout your life. It's the process of Knowing, rather then a fixed point (or even a two-point code) that's the real gift. But this foundational information can help you use that gift in powerful, life transforming ways.

Understanding the 20 Two-Point Intuitive Style Codes

In understanding the 20 patterns of intuitive style explained below, keep in mind that the most prominent form of intuition is listed first. People with scores very close to each other will find that the differentiations between the two components are not as sharply defined. That means that in actual practice, determining "which came first" may be frustrating at times. In such situations, bear in mind that as long as your intuition is reinforcing itself through the use of more than one sensory channel, its reliability and accuracy is improving. So, "which came first" is not that important; worry about how you use your intuition more and how it works less as you develop fluency with your personal intuitive language.

Visual-Auditory: This intuitive style is one of the most common, probably because we depend so much our sight and our hearing for our understanding of the world. People with this pattern tend to be dismissive of their intuition, probably because it relies so much on their most-used senses. The visual component is usually perceived first, but not always. People with this Intuitive Style can easily train themselves to use their intuition more effectively because often the world around them provides feedback which further strengthens their ability to trust their intuition.

Visual-Sensory: Learning to understand the body's wisdom will help people with this particular Intuitive Style become effective in their application of their intuition. Very often people with this type of intuition get a "double dose" because their body signals reinforce their visual cues, often nearly simultaneously. An example is when a person awakes from a dream of someone who has died, feeling a strong sense of the individual in the bedroom.

Visual-Gut/Body-Based: People who report this type of intuitive style often experience gut/body-based signals following their initial visual intuitive insights. It's very easy to dismiss both visual cues (*of course I saw my father's name on that street sign; it's not that surprising*) and body-based signals (*Sure, I felt a tug in my heart when that happened, but it's probably just indigestion*). The combination of signs is what causes people to realize that they have been receiving intuitive signals all along but have been dismissing them.

Visual-Mixed: This intuitive style is one that many people develop over time, first by relying on their Visual Intuition and then by using other building blocks of their intuitive style to reinforce or reinterpret the symbolism they're receiving. This pattern is often seen in highly artistic or creative people and those who make time for meditation and other quiet pursuits which allow them understand their body's signals coming from many sensory channels.

Auditory-Visual: This intuitive style is reported most by those who feel guided by an inner voice. In this case, their visual cues support their Auditory Intuition, so that they might first hear a voice and then see a confirming sign visually, often in the world around them. I know a woman who first hears clear guidance but also asks for a visual signal, because she's learned that asking for more will provide more. Her confirming visual signal is her birth date, often month, day, and year. The stigma against "hearing voices" keeps many people from acknowledging the way the process their intuitive cues, yet it's a commonly reported type of intuition through history.

Auditory-Sensory: This intuitive style is common among people who are not noted for being strongly visual observers of the world. If you've ever joked that a friend of yours wouldn't notice for three days if you dyed your hair purple, he might be more Auditory-Sensory. This is also the type of person who will ask, "What's wrong?" just from the tone of your voice over the telephone, sometimes before you've even spoken. They combine a sense of hearing a telepathic voice with a subtle awareness of changes in the energy field around them.

Auditory-Gut/Body-Based: This pattern of intuitive style is most commonly a situational response rather than an intuitive style that is experienced for long periods of time. Some people receive guidance on the auditory channel while also feeling a strong visceral, body-based reaction. An example is hearing a voice while driving that you warns to stop, while noticing a clutch in the stomach, a pain in the neck, or some other deeply body-based sensation. Often, it's the gut feeling rather than the auditory guidance that prompts people to act. That's because we're so used to hearing the voice of our own thoughts that we don't respond to it as strongly. The "push" of the gut/body-based aspect of this form of intuition pushes people into action.

Auditory-Mixed: This type of intuitive style is often found in people who are fond of the written and spoken word as well as in the musically inclined. The other intuitive channels flesh out the voice of auditory intuitive guidance. As with any form of Mixed Intuition, the Auditory-Mixed intuitive style is more common among those who create time in their lives to calm and quiet the mind, so that they can perceive the subtle voices of spiritual guidance.

Sensory-Visual: People who are strongly sensory-visual in their intuitive style are those who first receives subtle signs that something is wrong in the "field." Then their visual cues click in to either confirm or disconfirm that sense. As people become more adept at trusting their Sensory Intuition, they find that this loop of sensory perception/visual confirmation or disconfirmation/revised perception happens so quickly that it often feels simultaneous.

Sensory-Auditory: This intuitive style felt first in the energy field around people and situations, and often includes emotional sensitivity, as does most Sensory Intuition. This intuitive style enables its possessors to feel before words are spoken whether a person they've just met is someone they can comfortably trust. Strong Sensory-Auditory Intuition enables a person to tune into the vibe that prompts him to find another location in which to rest when walking through a park or an airport. It's being able to read the "vibe" and respond to the follow-up guidance perceived as a telepathic voice. It's often the intuitive style of people who proudly state, "I'm a good judge of character."

Sensory-Gut/Body-Based: This intuitive style is among the most reported, probably because of our natural-born hard-wiring that provides us with the lifesaving fight-or-flight response that our ancestors relied upon. It's more commonly reported by men. Learning to attend to the body's intuitive signals can result in a wide range of life improvements, from reduced accident-prone behavior and improved athletic response to an enhanced ability to assess one's health status and take preventive action earlier.

Sensory-Mixed: This Intuitive Style is often found in people who are very aware of their movement—for example, athletes, dancers, and yoga practitioners. Kinesthetic learners and other people who are very "hands on" in their approach to life often display Sensory-Mixed Intuition.

Gut/Body-Based-Visual: People who report this type of intuitive style often experience body-based signals, although they may not recognize them initially. It's very easy to dismiss body-based signals, because they often mimic actual symptoms we might experience anyway. Then, the backup system of Visual Intuition kicks in, and the person realizes that he or she has been receiving intuitive signals all along.

Gut/Body-Based-Auditory: In this intuitive style, the body supplies the first intuitive signal from a deeper level than Sensory Intuition, which is felt from the skin out and is often a response to a disturbance in the energy field around a person or situation; this is a deeper physical response. If not interpreted properly, as a back-up, it may be followed by auditory intuitives signals. Often the two are experienced so closely together that either one is dismissed or missed completely.

Gut/Body-Based-Sensory: This combination is a very powerful one, often seen in people who consider themselves as skeptics. They don't want to misinterpret anything they see or hear, which is admirable. Sometimes eye witnesses to the same event can't agree that the car was blue or green. We all make mistakes of interpretation of sensory data, so watch the pattern rather than any single detail. People with Gut/Body-Based-Sensory Intuition receive their signals physically and often attribute them to other causes because they haven't learned to translate the information. For that reason, people with high degrees of this type of intuition will often claim they have no intuitive awareness at all; people in this group also are likely to report that they don't recall dreams.

Gut/Body-Based-Mixed: People reporting this intuitive style are the ones who get a "power hunch" and then see the theme repeated on other sensory channels. Generally they have learned to trust their gut when a particularly strong impression strikes. Even if they work to develop the more subtle intuitive channels, they will always find that when there's a serious problem, they'll feel it the way they always do: deep inside first, confirmed by other senses second.

Intuition and Efficiency

Intuition is amazing in its efficiency. It includes a built-in redundancy, like a backup system on your computer. Your intuition is designed to keep sending you information if your primary system—whatever your highest appraisal score shows—fails. You'll continue to receive intuitive signs until you can no longer overlook the synchronicities. But if you're interested in shortening the learning curve and getting more Aha! moments of pure, clear awareness, absolute Knowing, keep working with your natural-born intuition. And just as important, learn about your core values.

That's what we'll look at in Chapters 16 and 17. But in the next few chapters, I want to help you understand how Knowing and mediumship are connected, as well as how Knowing and trauma interact. Being able to assess connections to the past and discern connections to the Unseen World will clear a pathway for you that will take you even deeper into your Knowing Zone.

CHAPTER 14
TRAUMA, FEAR,
AND KNOWING

"Learn wisdom from the ways of a seedling. A seedling which is never hardened off through stressful situations will never become a strong productive plant."

—Stephen Sigmund

Knowing has it roots in trauma, because it's rooted in an instinctual fight-or-flight response. That near-death experiences trigger psychic sensitivity is well-documented. Young children are particularly sensitive to Body-Based Intuition, especially those in dangerous or life-threatening situations. Children must interpret the world long before they can speak. Before they can understand and interpret spoken, auditory, or visual data, they have their bodies, which provide important, reliable information: I'm hungry, I'm lonely, I'm happy, I'm cold, I'm frightened, I hurt, I'm bored, I have to poop.

While all children are highly intuitive, people who grow up in very unpredictable circumstances such as homes with alcoholic, drug-abusing, violent, sexually predatory, mentally ill, or otherwise unstable family members develop amazingly strong gifts of intuitive response, particularly gut/body-based intuitive response.

Because intuition at its core is a survival skill based on the fight-or-flight response to fear, and children in these circumstances are forced to muster all the resources they can to survive, strong intuition is a natural outgrowth of threatening, traumatic experiences. Most people consider highly developed intuition a gift, but, in far too many cases, it's a hard-won fight. This may be one reason so many adults shy away from using their intuition. Perhaps it reminds them on a deeply subconscious level of the reasons they developed strong intuition in the first place. They may choose not to look at that shadowy, dark side of their psyche where the pain that fostered their intuition resides; poking around in this particular basement is still too scary.

Sexual abuse trauma alone has a far-reaching impact on the development of intuition. Because studies routinely indicate that as many as 1/3 of girls and 1/6 of boys in the United States are sexually abused by age 18, this represents a lot of people who have the potential to develop strong, Gut/Body-Based forms of Knowing. Add to this those people who grow up in homes with emotional or physical violence or with adults who have substance abuse problems and the number of people relying on their intuition as a necessity becomes a majority. Although such societal ills should certainly be addressed, one powerful trait developed in such traumatic circumstances is reliable Gut/Body-Based Intuition.

Intuition has played an important protective role in the lives of such people. In the world of psychology, this is often called hypervigilance, living with antenna always up. Imagine a 4-year-old child, wondering to himself, *Is this a good day to talk to Daddy?* In his own body, often from having made a choice which led to a negative experience, he'll Know. *Walking on eggs* so as not to upset an adult who's chronically on the verge of violent outbursts, whether emotional, physical, or sexual, is a daily experience in many households.

And it remains true throughout our lifetimes: Our bodies do tell us the truth. The important questions to ask include, "What is my body telling me? And why?" Very few of us check in with our bodies on a regular basis. We attribute physical symptoms to the outside world, to stress, to other people, when these symptoms may be our subconscious minds trying to cue us into a need for change in our lives. Our bodies are trying to guide us to a better life.

In addition to strong sensory intuition, a powerful resilience often develops in people who've had to pay constant attention to their environments in order to survive them. These are the folks who seem to always find a way, no matter what. They have a determination and a wonderful kind of practical optimism; to them, life will always be better than it used to be, no matter what happens. The most resilient people are those who've learned to view the experiences that led them to develop the responses of intuition and resilience as gifts—no matter how difficult they were. That's an amazingly powerful place in which to live. Like intuition, resilience is a lasting gift of a traumatic early life. Together, Intuition and resilience form a powerful foundation for inner wisdom.

Long before they realize that the people in their external world are unreliable, children in threatening environments Know that their bodies will tell them the truth, every time, unlike the adults around them. Their bodies are reliable assessors of what's going on around them. Even if they can't yet form the concept of intuitive insight, they Know their intuition is always right in that it wants to help them. This sets up appropriate conditions for developing reliable, life-long Body-Based Intuition, if they can learn to release and heal the pain of traumatic life experiences. Children in life-threatening environments must also avoid educating themselves too far into the left-brain dominant world we revere in modern Western culture.

If you're fortunate and did not have a traumatic early life—although everyone's life has its painful corners and memories—congratulations. While your intuition may be less obvious because you haven't needed it for your survival, you can learn to access both your natural-born intuition and your resilience. In fact, the two go together. As you learn to honor your own Knowing, which requires focusing on the Now, you will discover you're naturally less attached to a particular outcome. That means you're more flexible, and more resilient, much more willing to put your focus in a certain direction, but not a particular destination. You learn to honor the process, and appreciate the product, whatever it is. And often, it's better than you ever imagined.

We're Not Always Meant to Know

We are not always meant to Know in time to change an outcome we, as humans in the Earthly World, would like to avoid. The Unseen World is our teacher and sometimes the lessons are painful, leaving us wondering what clues we missed. Many people reported in the wake of the September 11, 2001, attacks in New York City that they'd had gut, body-based clues of imminent disaster, but weren't sure what they represented. Keep in mind that events that remain in the cultural consciousness, such as this one, are easy to look back on. And when we reflect, we often notice clues which we overlooked or explained away. I've done it myself.

On September 9, 2001, I was on a flight home from Atlanta, where I'd been conducting workshops. As the plane made a wide turn to land, the New York City skyline came into view. It was a perfectly beautiful late summer afternoon. The city sparkled.

I fly often enough that I rarely notice the skyline, but this time I set aside the book I was reading to appreciate a man across the aisle pointing out the tall buildings to his son, who was about 7 years old and clearly had never flown before. I followed along, witnessing the skyline for the first time through a child's eyes, smiling at the scene.

"That's the Empire State Building, see it? And that's the Statue of Liberty—you know that one, right? See those two tall black buildings? Those are the tallest ones in the United States. That's the World Trade Center."

As the man explained the skyline to his son, I had a moment of Knowing, which was primarily auditory but that also resonated in my solar plexus, just at the diaphragm. I felt like someone had punched me as I heard and felt very deeply these words: *It won't be like that for him.* I was completely calm, not unnerved, just quite aware, very much in the Knowing Zone.

But I ignored the information. My analytical left brain started up its commentary right away. Skylines change over time. It's logical, common knowledge. And who'd want to think about *why* a big city skyline might change, if it wasn't the typical old-buildings-come-down-new-ones-go-up scenario? Clearly I didn't. As I gathered my belongings, I mused rather absentmindedly, *Hmmm, that's interesting. I wonder what the skyline will look like when he's grown.*

My husband picked me up at the Newark airport and we headed home for dinner on the patio, fully enjoying the late afternoon sun on a perfect September day. Although I may have mentioned it to my husband on the ride home, I didn't think more about that sweet father-and-son interaction until about 40 hours later, when the tragedy occurred on September 11, 2001.

Why didn't I go deeper into this Knowing Moment? I didn't want to "go negative" I suppose. Anxiety and worry are choices we make, and generally I choose not to create either one. Also, I'm a pragmatist at heart: calling some authority would have no impact. Trust me when I say I learned that by experience; I'd Known about the 1986 Challenger explosion a few months prior to its occurrence and had placed a few ineffective calls to the NASA Lewis Research Center in Cleveland, where I lived.

So, had I honored that sense of Knowing about the 9/11 attacks and explored it more deeply, I would have lived with anxiety and worry, and the outcome would not have changed. I suppose on some level I Knew that, too, and dismissed an opportunity to Know more about the tragedy before it happened.

Many people in the wake of 9/11 have begun to plant the seeds of those changes, and others have reinvested themselves in the process of personal evolution. Doing so has powerful impacts; we all gain collectively from even small positive changes made by others. To change the course of human evolution, we first must change our own evolution.

The Impact of Trauma on Intuition

As mentioned previously, I've noticed that people who grow up in very unpredictable circumstances such as homes with alcoholic, drug-abusing, violent, sexually predatory, mentally ill, or otherwise unstable family members develop amazingly strong gifts of intuitive response. But why? They had to. Many people consider highly developed intuition a gift, but in many cases it's the result of a hard-won fight.

A client once taught me a great deal about the power of this fight. She'd been through traumas that included witnessing her mother's stabbing murder by her father at age 7. She then lived in a string of foster homes, some of which had been abusive environments, both sexually and physically. Robyn fought for and built a good life for herself in spite of her rough start, finishing college in record time, moving to a part of the country far from where these experiences had happened, buying her first home as a single woman of 27, and attending law school part-time at night.

She came to see me in large part because, as she neared 30, her trauma-inspired intuitive gifts were flourishing, although uncontrolled. Because she associated her strong psychic sensitivities with the pain of her early life, Robyn was understandably distressed. Accessing her intuition also brought up the painful memories of its source—traumatic life events. By helping her to unlink those associations and focus on the powerful spiritual gifts which flowered in the midst of her life traumas, eventually Robyn was able to relax about her intuition, further develop her Knowing, and put these gifts to work in her life in deliberate, structured ways. After all, she'd earned this power—why not use it? In her planned career in law, a strong psychic sense and insightful Knowing will be incredible assets. I won't be surprised to hear someday that Robyn became a criminal profiler or a forensic psychologist. She's found a way to heal her traumas and unveil the gifts wrapped in the pain of her early life.

Missing the Signs of Gut/Body-Based Intuition

People who choose to live in unenlightened ways are out there. They can and do touch your life. To help you deal with the "dark side" or "shadow side" of human nature, what I term unenlightened free-will choice, it's important to delve into your own dark places. We all have them. They're necessary for the human experience. Bringing them from that messy basement of your subconscious mind up into the light of your own Knowing will teach you how to live more fully, more freely, more richly, more gratefully. First, however, you may have some release work to do (see Chapter 10).

That release work requires you to go back to and fully feel the original stressor or cause of the traumatic, painful experience. This is not reliving old pain, but experiencing it from a more mature perspective and with greater life wisdom.

The traumas of our lives can become our greatest teachers if we are willing to see them as gifts wrapped in difficult experiences. If you struggle with this process—and many people do; it's one of most challenging aspects of developing inner wisdom—I encourage you to seek guidance and support from an appropriately credentialed psychotherapist, coach or other professional. You are worth the investment of time, energy, and funds in support of your wise and Knowing Self.

CHAPTER 15
MEDIUMSHIP
AND KNOWING

Working with Knowing, and particularly with Mixed Intuition and symbolic shorthand, often leads to an awakening of mediumship. Mediumship is a very specific form of Knowing that allows it to be extended on behalf of others through sharing messages from passed-on loved ones. In this way, the mediumship form of Knowing becomes very much a gift of healing for the recipient of the messages. And through the practice and focused development of this capability, you can develop an even stronger connection to your Knowing because often (although not always) mediumship messages are verifiable. Living in the Knowing Zone requires an ability to trust what you perceive, even when it cannot be verified. Still, verification enhances trust in your Knowing, and thus increases your capacity and comfort with this natural ability.

An excellent way to better understand symbolic shorthand and Mixed Intuition in Knowing is to watch a television programs or attend events featuring mediums demonstrating a particular type of Knowing called message mediumship, the most common type of Knowing demonstrated publicly today. John Edward of television's groundbreaking show *Crossing Over with John Edward* and James van Praagh of the program *Beyond with James van Praagh* are good examples. If you live near a Spiritualist camp or church (you'll find some listed on page 217), or find a venue where mediums come to speak or conduct workshops, consider attending simply to witness the process of mediumship. You can also watch or participate in chat room discussions and demonstrations of mediumship online at such sites as *SeekersCircle.com*. These memberships are often available for free or a reasonable fee.

As you witness message mediumship, watch for visual references which have specific meaning to the message-bearer, the Knower serving in the role of medium. For example, John Edward is open about his large brood of loving Italian family members. Each has a specific meaning to him, whether it's to point him toward a name, a condition, a relationship, or a shared memory with that loved one that will also be relevant to the message recipient. He knows his visual symbolic shorthand well, so seeing a brief flash of a relative's face is a cue from his symbolic shorthand that opens up the door to a powerful message for someone else. It comes through having a deeply honed sense of his own Knowing.

Keep in mind that Knowing is not about "being right" although good mediums generally are accurate 80 percent of the time (or more), which has been documented by researchers such as Gary Schwartz and Linda Russek at the University of Arizona. The power of Knowing truly is in the process, although messages can be very insightful, comforting, and healing to receive.

As you watch mediums working, take notes. Pay attention to when they're in what I call the M-zone, the mediumship zone or Knowing place where the mediums demonstrate an inner confidence about the messages they are presenting, even if the recipient is unable to completely understand the meaning right at that moment. Often, time passes before the full impact of a message is understood. Sometimes, the full impact is never understood.

Even so, you'll see that a medium operating from Knowing will not be dissuaded easily and will be more attached to the process than to a specific outcome. In other words, well-trained mediums will not mind being "wrong" in the moment. The reason? Knowing is as much about the medium trusting his or her own Knowing as it is about the message. Experienced mediums Know this. This is why practicing the ancient art of mediumship is one of the best ways to develop a deeper level of inner wisdom, of Knowing.

As you watch others perform mediumship, realize that your symbolic references and symbolic shorthand will be different. You'll have to pay attention and take notes to develop a good working understanding of your Knowing process. My family is quite small, so my messages rely on symbolic references and metaphorical symbols rather than references to family. I was never a big film fan, so I don't have the working understanding of film and television upon which some mediums rely. I've learned that my background and training in business and counseling offer me Knowing symbols unique to me. The symbols I use have evolved through time, as will yours, with focus and practice.

When I first began working in mediumship, seeing an image of coins in an open palm to me always meant that the person had been an entrepreneur. After a few years, this symbol began to evolve. Sometimes the coins would be silver. At other times, gold. Soon I learned the new meanings: silver coins represented a coin collector, gold coins represented a business owner. Additional symbols were added to further inform me about the message being conveyed. Now the image of an old-fashioned green ledger account book tells me it was a family business, begun in the days before computers were ubiquitous, and that it either suffered through extremely hard times or closed completely. Silver coins moving through the air above an open hand tell me that a person was fond of sleight-of-hand magic tricks such as card and coin tricks for entertainment. A magician shows himself to me with the classic upturned black hat, complete with rabbit emerging. The process of Knowing involves paying attention to your symbols. It's not only instructive, it's fun. And it's all based on *you*.

Empowerment Through Training

Training your Knowing is critical because it encourages you to develop a deep place of inner trust, the M-zone, that Knowing place, which leads to a profound self-empowerment. While exercises such as predicting the color of next car to go through the intersection are valuable because they are an immediate feedback loop. This immediate feedback means that the journey of Knowing, which often requires the passage of time, can be overlooked. Making a connection to your own Knowing to that Unseen World represented by the upper loop of a figure eight (see page 17), requires deep trust and a faith in yourself—and your ability to connect with the larger world outside yourself. Sitting with your Knowing is not easy to do in a now-now-now, instant gratification society like ours (we don't even use the one-hour photo service much anymore, because we can use our cell phones as cameras).

In the same way that scientists may first notice trends and patterns about how the world operates and then formulate hypotheses to test their observations, we are becoming better at documenting patterns of Knowing. Even though your patterns of Knowing and your symbolic shorthand differ from everyone else, common threads exist. One of those common threads is that all people have the capacity to work mediumistically, to perceive information from the Unseen World beyond this one.

Another common thread is that, as with any human endeavor or possibility, skill levels vary dramatically. Just as human intelligence or musical skill covers a wide range, so does the capacity for Knowing—and for being duped. You must be discerning about mediumship and strive for detail; Generalities won't do.

Your Evolving Symbolic Shorthand

As you keep your Knowing Journey Journal, you'll want to pay attention to the evolution of the signs and symbols you receive. As happens with me and countless other mediums I've worked with over the years, the symbols expand, developing subtle meanings that shift and grow along with your depth of understanding.

Over the many years I've worked as a medium, I've had many good days and some not-so-great days before crowds numbering in the many hundreds and larger. Although the goal is always to present accurate, easily understood messages that make immediate sense, several things work against that outcome. One is the expectations among the audience members. Nearly all have a specific someone from whom they most hope to hear. They want to make whatever information they receive fit their expectations and desires, which actually clouds the message. Another thing that works against the clarity of the messages is the audience members' inability to recall whom they're related to or have interacted with over the course of a lifetime. We touch many lives in our interactions, and may not even recall how much we meant to someone else who's passed on. But those who have passed on do.

I still remember once presenting a message many years ago to a woman in a large crowd on a summer afternoon in Lily Dale, New York, a large Spiritualist center near Buffalo, New York, active since 1879. She was probably in her early 70s. I told her I felt the presence of a woman with her who had taught her to plink around a bit on the piano, holding her on her lap when she was quite young. I also felt that when she was about 5 years old, she'd held this woman's hand as she took her last breath, succumbing to heart failure. She felt to me like non-blood-related aunt or family friend.

This feisty lady assured me (and about 600 other audience members) that I was absolutely wrong, that this had never happened. She clearly felt that I was making up a tear-jerker story and communicated that quite clearly through her "this-is-a-crock" demeanor, complete with crossed arms and side-to-side head-shaking.

This is not exactly the type of mediumship message you want to witness if you're a person who likes neat tidy messages that wrap up within two minutes, an artificial constraint imposed by public demonstration venues like Lily Dale and television and radio programs. If you're a medium, it's not the type you like to give, either. Loose ends are not educational. But they happen.

I did my best to shrug it off as I headed back down the stone path out of the woods to meet my afternoon clients. The woman suddenly called out to me. She'd followed me and was crying.

"I know who that is," she said through joyful tears of recognition. "I haven't thought about the woman I called Aunt Edith in more than 60 years. But she was my mother's boarder during the Depression, when we rented out a bedroom in our home. It's true: she did teach me to play a bit of piano, and I was the only one with her when she died. I was 5 years old."

Through a single moment of Knowing that I shared with her, the woman's hard edge had shifted to a softness I'd never have associated with her before. I felt honored that she'd sought me out to say, "I understand now."

✶✶✶✶

Sometimes accurate information is brought through that cannot (or will not) be verified. There is a valid reason why we use the term *family secrets*. Other times people simply blank on their family histories, or are unwilling to have personal information (however well intended), brought into a public forum.

I still laugh remembering a lovely family, three generations of strong, proud Jewish women who came to see me as a group of five. The grandmother was in her 80s, quite deaf, and a vision in her lavender ruffle neckline cashmere sweater and eggplant-purple trousers which set off her silver hair and clear blue eyes. Her two daughters and two grand-daughters had a longing to connect with a woman, their daughter/sister/mother/aunt, who'd died of breast cancer in her early 50s. In addition to a joyful reunion with this woman, the Lady in Purple's father arrived on the scene. He announced that his second wife, this elderly woman's mother, was with him, clearly inferring that he'd indeed had two wives. The other four women immediately and loudly contested this. "Grandpa Howard never had two wives! He was devoted to our grandmother!" They chattered on for a bit, as I stayed in the M-zone, very clearly aware from Howard that, yes, he'd been married and divorced before he found his true love in his second wife.

Finally the regal Lady in Purple said, "Well, I never told you, it was a family secret until today, but it's true. My father Howard was married and divorced before he married my mother." The dropped jaws and "What!? Tell us the whole story!" responses led, I'm sure, to a lively discussion on the ride home.

Just recently a woman I'd met more than 15 years ago in a meditation circle told me that a message I'd given her then, about her mother's true parentage, had led her on a journey of discovery that foreged powerful bonds with previously unacknowledged branches of her family more than 2,500 miles away as well as overseas.

Why do these kinds of experiences happen in consultations with mediums? For at least two good reasons.

The first is that it reinforces the power of connection to the Unseen World for the recipients. If they had not known certain truths about a family member or friend, when a medium addresses it through Knowing, it's clear that the information was drawn from outside the mind of the recipient (as well as the medium).

The second is that in the wake of such an experience, people often admit that they never felt they'd had the "whole story" in the first place. It confirms their *own* Knowing, which can be a life-changing moment.

A similar experience led me to work with a police detective after family members and friends of a murdered man offered tapes of our years-earlier sessions to aid in the investigation when it was assigned to him as a "cold" or long-unsolved case. Material known only to the detective was discussed on those tapes, which led us to work together on a research project about mediumship and crime.

Worries about so-called "mind reading" are put to rest in circumstances such as these because the message recipient himself doesn't hold the information in mind. This means that the information must be coming from somewhere outside the parties involved. As a result, the seeds of a new way of looking at life, from a larger perspective, are planted.

Working with skilled, experienced mediums in ongoing development circles will bring out your innate gifts of mediumship. Mediumship resources are found on pages 217-218.

CHAPTER 16
VALUES AND INTUITION:
THE EMPOWERING CONNECTION

"Intuition and concepts constitute...the elements of all our knowledge, so that neither concepts without an intuition in some way corresponding to them nor intuition without concepts, can yield knowledge."

—*Immanuel Kant*

Your intuition works hand in hand with your personal value system. Where your heart goes, your intuition follows. If you're passionate about animals, then your natural-born intuition will be even more effective in that realm. If you're passionate about health and wellness, then your natural intuitive style will lead you to deep and powerful Knowing in that arena. Your Knowing is built on your natural intuitive style as well as your values. You must be able to voice your values, to understand what really matters to *you.* Clearing away the clutter of others' dreams for us, society's expectations of us, or the guilt we sometimes feel for seeking our own truth is often the biggest obstacle we face to becoming Knowing beings.

Taking time to assess, perhaps for the first time, what you truly want from life will bring you closer to your soul's purpose—the one thing that your Knowing keeps prompting you toward, no matter what. Yes, resistance is possible, but, as the familiar saying states, it is futile.

As water flowing downstream, when one course is blocked, the water will always find another route. *Always.* As water flowing downhill, your Knowing won't be dissuaded. Your Knowing inner wisdom gently, persistently, flows toward what's best for you, or, it goes underground, becoming a deep well waiting until you're ready to tap its resources, as you're doing now by working with this book.

If you've taken a meandering course in life, relax. "Go with the flow" and your journey through life will be more straightforward, more efficient, and less stressful in many ways. But where's the fun in that? I'd have skipped a multitude of interesting life adventures if I'd followed the natural course of things earlier on, and you probably would have, too. The flow of your intuition, your Knowing, is always toward the highest and best situation, even when it detours around obstacles, beomes a destructive flood at points, or goes underground. And all that life experience adds to your values, which is a critical element of Knowing.

Focusing on what you want in any situation makes achieving the highest and best result that much easier. This process of inquiry and self-awareness will empower your Knowing so that it becomes a reliable, effective life guidance tool. Learning to read the currents of that flowing water on your Inward Journey to your Knowing Self makes you the captain of your soul.

Voice Your Values: Seven Key Considerations

The following Voice Your Values exercise is a good place to start your Inward Journey to better understanding how your intuition and your values work together to bring your Knowing forth. You can either read the statements out loud and state your responses into a recording device, or work with a pen and paper. Voice in this case is either literal or symbolic—just like your Knowing symbolism.

Find a comfortable, relaxing environment for the following exercise. Allow about 15 to 30 minutes. If you don't finish, that's fine. You can complete it later. It's not a "test" with a time limit, but a process of personal inquiry.

Complete the following seven statements. These are key considerations in unearthing your life's purpose, because values are tied so critically to your Knowing Self. Feel free to provide more than one answer, or to use your Knowing Journal to write more. If you become "stuck" on any statement, take it with you into meditation, or focus on it before sleeping so that your meditation and dream states can offer insights to consider. Those are the times when the mind is most relaxed.

1. The time I value most is spent _____.
2. The person(s) I value most is/are/were _____.
3. My fondest dream for my future is that I _____.
4. When I think back on my life to this point, I'm surprised by _____.
5. The phrase or saying that guides me most is _____.
6. Others value me for my _____.
7. If money didn't matter and no one would judge me, I would spend my life _____.

As you scan your responses to the previous seven key consideration statements, notice any patterns or repeated themes. Do you see repeated references to caretaking? To curiosity and inquiry? To education? Science? Sports? Travel? Computers? Arts? Business pursuits? A desire for solitude or a different living environment completely?

Jot key phrases down in your Knowing Journal so you'll remember them easily and have them for future reference. They may change over time as you go through different phases of your life, so you may wish to retake this self-assessment every few months, and then review your responses over time to see what larger themes emerge (other useful queries can be found in Appendix C).

The next section takes a little more time to complete, but I promise you, it's a learning journey worth the investment. The Values-by-Color Inventory was developed to help you understand what motivates you, and just as importantly, what *demotivates* you. The things that move you forward you may already understand very well. But the things that hold you back—that's an entirely different story. You'll need about an hour to complete it if you want to take all seven sections in one sitting. I Know you have the time: you've spent more time than that shopping for shoes, playing video games, aimlessly surfing the Internet, or waiting at the airport.

However, if you prefer, complete one section a day for a week in about 10 minutes each day; it's an ideal way to spend your last cup of tea or a portion of your lunch break. After you complete the assessment, you'll be directed to chart the results to complete your Knowing Self-Portrait on page 195, which shows you how your Knowing Self operates at this point in your life.

For all seven sections of the Values-by-Color Inventory, use this scale to determine what number to choose.

4: **Passionately important:** I devote a lot of mental or physical energy to this; it is a passion.

3: **Very Important:** I consider this important, but I would not say I am passionate about it.

2: **Fairly Important:** I give this a fair amount of attention.

1: **Sometimes Important:** I put energy into this sometimes.

0: **Not Important:** This is of no interest to me whatsoever.

-1: **De-motivator:** Just reading this statement de-motivates me or makes feel energetically drained.

Now, look for any repeated words or "themes" you jotted down as you reacted to taking each section of the Values-by-Color Inventory.

Section 1 :   De-Motivator   Passion

#	Statement	De-Motivator / Passion
1.	Material wealth matters to me.	-1 0 1 2 3 4
2.	Adventure sports matter to me.	-1 0 1 2 3 4
3.	Owning my own home matters to me.	-1 0 1 2 3 4
4.	Working out for the feeling it gives me matters to me (looking better is a bonus).	-1 0 1 2 3 4
5.	Living a long time matters to me.	-1 0 1 2 3 4
6.	Competitive sports and games, including computer games, matter to me.	-1 0 1 2 3 4
7.	Keeping my current job/profession, even if it's not my dream, matters to me.	-1 0 1 2 3 4
8.	Having a financially secure retirement matters to me.	-1 0 1 2 3 4
9.	Having children to continue the family lineage matters to me.	-1 0 1 2 3 4
10.	Having family to take care of me in old age matters to me.	-1 0 1 2 3 4
11.	Keeping my hometown roots no matter where I move matters to me.	-1 0 1 2 3 4
12.	Managing my weight successfully matters to me.	-1 0 1 2 3 4

13.   Staying with my current employer, for the
      benefits and security, matters to me.   -1 0 1 2 3 4
14.   Looking young matters to me enough that I
      would undergo painful plastic surgery if I had
      the extra funds to do so.   -1 0 1 2 3 4

Section total (add all positive numbers first, then count off any -1s. _____

Add a few key words or sentences about how you felt taking Section 1 of this assessment here. _____

Section 2:	De-Motivator	Passion

1.   Enjoying or preparing great-tasting or
      gourmet foods matters to me.   -1 0 1 2 3 4
2.   Being in a sexually charged relationship,
      even if it's not forever or commitment-minded,
      matters to me.   -1 0 1 2 3 4
3.   Creating or enjoying beautiful surroundings that
      appeal to my senses matter to me.   -1 0 1 2 3 4
4.   Expressing my emotions through discussion with
      friends and family matters to me.   -1 0 1 2 3 4
5.   Indulging myself in bodily pleasures such as massage,
      spa treatments, etc. matters to me.   -1 0 1 2 3 4
6.   Having a life partner or spouse for the long term
      matters to me.   -1 0 1 2 3 4
7.   Participating in dance, yoga, martial arts, tai chi,
      or other fluid, artistic movement matters to me. -1 0 1 2 3 4
8.   Sharing my feelings by journaling or writing them
      down matters to me.   -1 0 1 2 3 4
9.   Feeling free to become angry if I need to matters to me. -1 0 1 2 3 4
10.   Releasing frustrations at those who have contributed
      to my irritation matters to me.   -1 0 1 2 3 4
11.   Clothing that feels good against my skin matters to me. -1 0 1 2 3 4
12.   Having dessert or other "treat" foods when I need a reward
      or to feel better matters to me.   -1 0 1 2 3 4
13.   Experiencing sexual release and/or romantic physical
      affection with a partner on a regualr basis matters to me. -1 0 1 2 3 4
14.   Traveling to relax and regroup, rather than to sightsee
      or learn new things, matters to me.   -1 0 1 2 3 4

Section total (add all positive numbers first, then count off any -1s.) _____

Add a few key words or sentences about how you felt taking Section 2 of this assessment here. _____

Section 3:

		De-Motivator	Passion

1. Having a work role where I'm in charge
    (including self-employment or entrepreneurship)
    matters to me.   -1 0 1 2 3 4
2. Knowing others value my talents matters to me.   -1 0 1 2 3 4
3. Working to achieve goals matters to me—the
    outcome is as important as the process.   -1 0 1 2 3 4
4. Being respected as a parent (or leader in my circle
    of family and friends if not a parent) matters to me.   -1 0 1 2 3 4
5. Making my own decisions without a lot of input
    from others matters to me.   -1 0 1 2 3 4
6. Having friends from a variety of professions from
    whom I can get ideas, support, and help matters to me.   -1 0 1 2 3 4
7. Building connections that can help me in my career
    or profession matters to me.   -1 0 1 2 3 4
8. Creating opportunities to assist or mentor others, in
    work or leisure pursuits, matters to me.   -1 0 1 2 3 4
9. Hearing others tell me that I contribute meaningfully
    to their lives matters to me.   -1 0 1 2 3 4
10. Being spontanious and ready to try anything matters to me. -1 0 1 2 3 4
11. Winning formal recognition and achievements in my
    work, education, and hobbies matters to me.   -1 0 1 2 3 4
12. Writing, recording, or telling my life story to my
    family, friends, or others matters to me.   -1 0 1 2 3 4
13. Determining my fate in life matters to me; I believe
    it's really all up to me to create the life I want.   -1 0 1 2 3 4
14. Leaving my mark on the world matters to me.   -1 0 1 2 3 4

Section total (add all positive numbers first, then count off any -1s.) _____

Add a few key words or sentences about how you felt taking Section 3 of
this assessment here. _____

Section 4:   De-Motivator   Passion

1. Nurturing others as a parent, friend, or
   professional or workplace mentor matters to me.   -1 0 1 2 3 4

2. Being with people socially on a regular basis
   matters to me.   -1 0 1 2 3 4

3. Doing kindesses for friends and family members
   "just because" matters to me.   -1 0 1 2 3 4

4. Having a spouse or romantic partner who routinely
   shows me affection and love matters to me.   -1 0 1 2 3 4

5. Helping others matters to me enough that I
   volunteer my time regularly.   -1 0 1 2 3 4

6. Keeping the same circle of friends over the
   years matters to me.   -1 0 1 2 3 4

7. Sending out loving thoughts for the benefit of
   others matters enough that I pray or send distant
   healing regularly.   -1 0 1 2 3 4

8. Having friends I can call on at any time for support
   and encouragement matters to me.   -1 0 1 2 3 4

9. Socializing at parties and events where I don't
   know many people but can make new friends
   matters to me.   -1 0 1 2 3 4

10. Being perceived as a trustworthy friend, even when
    others seem to take advantage of my kindness,
    matters to me.   -1 0 1 2 3 4

11. Welcoming new people to my neighborhood,
    community of friends and family, and/or workplace
    matters to me.   -1 0 1 2 3 4

12. Demonstrating to others that I'm willing to listen,
    even when we disagree, matters to me.   -1 0 1 2 3 4

13. Accepting myself just as I am matters to me.   -1 0 1 2 3 4

14. Building many friendships with a wide range of people
    from many different backgrounds matters to me.   -1 0 1 2 3 4

Section total (add all positive numbers first, then count off any -1s.) _____

Add a few key words or sentences about how you felt taking Section 4 of
this assessment here. _____

Section 5:   De-Motivator   Passion

1. Telling others what I think about things,
    whether in conversation or via e-mail or
    correspondence, matters to me.   -1 0 1 2 3 4
2. Creative pursuits such as writing, musical
    performance, art, crafts, or drama matter to me.   -1 0 1 2 3 4
3. Finding an intellectual passion matters to me.   -1 0 1 2 3 4
4. Speaking up for what is right, even at personal
    cost, matters to me.   -1 0 1 2 3 4
5. "Just doing nothing" now and then matters to me.   -1 0 1 2 3 4
6. Clearly communicating what I'm about to new
    acquaintances in my work and leisure life
    matters to me.   -1 0 1 2 3 4
7. Resonating to something outside myself that
    makes me feel part of a greater whole matters to me.   -1 0 1 2 3 4
8. Mental quiet, even if I'm not meditating but just
    so I can think better, matters to me.   -1 0 1 2 3 4
9. Being what some call a lifelong learner—always
    trying new things—matters to me.   -1 0 1 2 3 4
10. Clearly and deeply understanding concepts and ideas
    so I can be sure of where I stand matters to me.   -1 0 1 2 3 4
11. Connecting deeply with like-minded people on an
    intellectual or idea/conceptual level matters to me.   -1 0 1 2 3 4
12. Cultivating an ability to appreciate the arts as an
    educated observer matters to me.   -1 0 1 2 3 4
13. Hearing from longstanding friends and acquaintences,
    even if we've lost touch for more than a few years,
    matters to me.   -1 0 1 2 3 4
14. A practice of regular meditation or quiet time
    matters to me.   -1 0 1 2 3 4

Section total (add all positive numbers first, then count off any -1s.) _____

Add a few key words or sentences about how you felt taking Section 5 of
this assessment here. _____

Section 6:	De-Motivator	Passion
1. Regularly evaluating the choices I've made in life matters to me.	-1 0 1 2 3 4	
2. Allowing my imagination free reign matters to me.	-1 0 1 2 3 4	
3. Developing my psychic and/or spiritual nature matters to me.	-1 0 1 2 3 4	
4. Talking over philosophical issues with others matters to me.	-1 0 1 2 3 4	
5. Learning more about metaphysics and psychic issues matters to me.	-1 0 1 2 3 4	
6. Keeping my memory sharp through memory exercises or other practice matters to me.	-1 0 1 2 3 4	
7. Understanding the world views of others matters to me.	-1 0 1 2 3 4	
8. Exchanging ideas through intellectual discussion matters to me.	-1 0 1 2 3 4	
9. Keeping up with emerging trends in spiritual thinking matters to me.	-1 0 1 2 3 4	
10. Reading well reviewed nonfiction books matters to me.	-1 0 1 2 3 4	
11. Avoiding deteriorating eyesight through exercises, surgery, or other means matters to me.	-1 0 1 2 3 4	
12. Seeking imaginative or innovative ideas matters to me.	-1 0 1 2 3 4	
13. Self-refelection matters to me.	-1 0 1 2 3 4	
14. Using my intuition regularly matters to me.	-1 0 1 2 3 4	

Section total (add all positive numbers first, then count off any -1s.) _____

Add a few key words or sentences about how you felt taking Section 6 of this assessment here. _____

Section 7:   De-Motivator   Passion

1.   Remaining unattached to the outcome
      of choices I make matters to me.   -1 0 1 2 3 4
2.   Developing true wisdom matters to me; I am a "seeker."   -1 0 1 2 3 4
3.   Bringing important issues to light for discussion
      matters to me.   -1 0 1 2 3 4
4.   Understanding universal principles to live
      by matters to me.   -1 0 1 2 3 4
5.   Studying with spiritual teachers matters to me.   -1 0 1 2 3 4
6.   The process of learning matters to me.   -1 0 1 2 3 4
7.   Finding others to challenge my understanding
      and push me to know more matters to me.   -1 0 1 2 3 4
8.   Understanding principles and ideas that others
      don't matters to me.   -1 0 1 2 3 4
9.   Letting go of material goods and attachments
      matters to me.   -1 0 1 2 3 4
10.   Seeking knowledge for its own sake matters to me.   -1 0 1 2 3 4
11.   Working with my "shadow side"—parts of myself
      I may not like—matters to me.   -1 0 1 2 3 4
12.   Knowing that I make a difference in the world
      or will leave a legacy one day matters to me.   -1 0 1 2 3 4
13.   Developing my consciousness fully matters to me.   -1 0 1 2 3 4
14.   How to know things better matters to me; I'm
      quite curious by nature.   -1 0 1 2 3 4

Section total (add all positive numbers first, then count off any -1s.) _____

Add a few key words or sentences about how you felt taking Section 7 of this assessment here. _____

This is important information that helps you understand the feelings triggered by considering different sets of personal values. Those to which you respond quite positively, negatively, or with a sense of confusion are sections to which you should pay particular attention as you continue your Inward Journey.

Here's how to score your Values by Color Inventory.

Letter/Color Association	Values by Color Section	Section Scores
R red	Section 1 score (see page 158):	
Y yellow	Section 2 score (see page 158):	
O orange	Section 3 score (see page 159):	
G green	Section 4 score (see page 160):	
B blue	Section 5 score (see page 161):	
I indigo	Section 6 score (see page 162):	
V violet	Section 7 score (see page 163):	

Write your three highest scores in order, highest to lowest, here:

_____   _____   _____

(the highest possible score on any section is 56; double-check your math)
Write the letters associated with each of those three scores here:

_____   _____   _____

Now, create an alpha-numeric code—it's easy—to reference your score pattern using the number from the top line followed by the letter from the bottom line, directly beneath it. Here is an example of an alphanumeric code:

49B 43Y 39R

The represents the highest score with its associated color code letter, the 2nd highest score with its associated color code letter, and the 3rd highest score with its associated color code letter. If you have two scores of the same numeric value, go back to the page for those sections and review them. Use the score with the fewest 0s and 1s as the default "higher" score.

For easy reference and use on your Knowing Self Portrait (see Appendix A) this code should be shortened to the letters only—BYR—which stands for Blue/Yellow/Red.

After you complete the Values-by-Color Inventory, you can place your codes on your Knowing Self-Portrait on page 195, which also indicates the primary seven chakras (or basic vibrational energy centers) as they are associated with the five basic building blocks of Intuitive Style. You can also transfer the scores from the five appraisals that make up your natural intuitive style (Visual, page 39; Auditory, page 60; Sensory, page 80; Gut/Body-Based, page 98, and Mixed, page 115, or see page 131 for your results summary).

This process provides a picture of how your Intuitive Style and your chakra colors, representing your values, line up to create your Knowing Self at this juncture in your life. This allows you to observe the levels to which you resonate naturally and which areas are less in alignment so you can awaken and develop them if you choose.

In the next chapter, we'll consider alignment between your Intuitive Style and your Values-by-Color Inventory more closely and offer ways for you to develop a more fully balanced profile. The more closely your intuitive style aligns with your values, and the better-rounded your profile, the more easily you'll be able to transform it into that amazing autopilot sense of guidance, Knowing.

Chapter 17
Colors, Values, and You

"You don't want a million answers as much as you want a few forever questions. The questions are diamonds you hold in the light. Study a lifetime and you see different colors from the same jewel."

—Richard Bach

Your Values-by-Color Inventory results can help you understand your level of consciousness and spiritual development, and guide you further into that Knowing Zone, where your inner wisdom leads you toward your greatest fulfillment in life. To better understand your color pattern, a basic understanding of the subtle energy system of the human body is necessary. The colors of the rainbow—red, orange, yellow, green, blue, indigo blue, and violet—are also the colors of the seven primary chakras. While there are over 10 million colors, you'll find that dealing just with the ones seen in a prism or rainbow opens up your Knowing. Over time, you'll expand your color symbolism.

Each chakra (a Sanskit word meaning "wheel" and pronounced shock-rah) corresponds to a body-based center of consciousness. The Knowing Self-Portrait in Appendix A indicates the seven basic chakra points. These seven main chakra points run along the spine from the tailbone to the crown. Each point represents a different kind or quality of subtle energy, and is represented by a different color. This subtle color energy can be focused and activated by various practices such as meditation and yoga. Activation of the chakras is sometimes referred to as kundalini rising or opening.

Color and Consciousness

Still with me? Good. Because it's important to the Knowing Process that you are familiar with your current level of consciousness. That "baseline" level is shown on the Knowing Self-Portrait on page 195 comprised of your Intuitive Style Inventory results and your Values-by-Color Inventory results. As you look at your Knowing Self-Portrait, you'll see that the upper five chakra colors correspond with the Intuitive Style Inventory results. Mixed Intuition lines up across from violet and Sensory Intuition across from green, for example.

A person whose Values-by-Color results indicate a predominance of red (a color that suggests a deep concern about security, safety, and the body) and who also shows a powerful degree of Mixed Intuition (Violet) may actually feel very disconnected from his or her intuition. That's because there's a big "gap" between the levels. But by deliberately working to develop his or her intuition, such a person would learn to bridge the gap, to build a reliable connection to his or her own Knowing by paying closer attention to the body's signals.

As you review your Knowing Self-Portrait, notice whether your natural intuitive style is in alignment with your Values-by-Color Inventory results. While that alignment is not necessarily a goal for which to strive, it does help you "see" what you're dealing with while you're becoming familiar with your Knowing. If you take the Intuitive Style Inventory and the Values-by-Color Inventory again in several months after working with your intuition, you're quite likely to see shifts and changes in the patterns, which indicate your growth from the baseline patterns.

Whether or not you have large gaps or "holes" in your Knowing Self-Portrait, there's information about you to be gleaned. If there's a small gap (or no gap) between your Values-by-Color and Intuitive Style results, you may want to extend yourself to new areas of conscious awareness and Knowing by developing other aspects of your intuition. If you've ever been accused of needing to be more grounded, you'll appreciate that having wide-open awareness at the upper range of the rainbow (indigo and violet) means it's tougher to get insights about the physical body and what it needs, although spiritual insight will be strong.

Whatever your results, you can use the information as a baseline from which to track your efforts and results.

Color has long been used in healing and has been tracked to Ancient Egypt, India, and Babylon. The physical body (gross anatomy) reflects the state of the spiritual/emotional body (subtle anatomy). By focusing on the chakras, we can release blocked energy even uncover physical and emotional problems.

The colors in your subtle energy field, also called the aura, shift and change all the time. Your level of consciousness, evidenced by the aura colors you show the world, shifts and changes as you actively work on your ability to use your natural-born intuition. Deliberate focus on bringing more of a particular color energy will help you direct those changes more successfully, and you'll have an entire rainbow of possibilities to access for your deepest Knowing.

Use Your Intuition

While the following information is generally agreed upon, you will, no doubt, come across books and speakers who interpret the chakra meanings differently. Use your own judgment, your own Knowing, to determine what interpretation is right for you. Color is a form of spiritual shorthand, so what the seven primary chakra colors mean to *you* is far more important than sticking to someone else's schema. And as your self-awareness expands and your Knowing evolves, the meanings you ascribe to certain colors may change, becoming more textured, subtle, and embedded with meaning.

The Red Zone: The First Chakra

Located at the base of the spine at the tailbone, the root (base) chakra resonates to the color red. This chakra governs perception of the physical world, things that "ground" us to the Earthly World. Base chakra energy also deals with will, motivation, intent and survival. Our fight-or-flight response is governed by the root chakra. It controls the adrenal gland, the kidneys, and the spinal column. In color healing, red is associated with blood, passion for life, regeneration, recuperation, stress management, chaos, anger, violence, courage, the womb and menstruation cycle, circulation, and fevers.

Red Zone Power Points Exercise

Find something red to hold, ideally something from nature, such as a flower, leaf, or feather. As you sit with this red object for at least five minutes, allow yourself to feel where in your body you resonate to this object. How does the object make you feel emotionally? Try a few different objects, including something man-made, and see how your connection varies. Write about your experience in your Knowing Journal.

The Orange Zone: The Second Chakra

The second or sexual chakra resonates to the color orange. Located in the center of the abdomen about a hand's-breadth below the navel (roughly the center of the uterus in a woman), the second chakra deals with the reproductive organs, sexuality, sexual identity, and sexual expression (or lack of it). In color healing, orange is associated with shock, trauma, beauty, sexuality, trust, deep insight, codependency, independence, harmony, ecstasy, devotion, wisdom, indecision, patience, hysteria, depression, ovaries, spleen, intestines, and the gall bladder. It governs the sexual organs, the kidneys and bladder. The orange chakra also deals with expressing the creative self creatively. The second chakra is the place where we are nourished and sheltered during fetal development, so life energy is strongly associated with the color orange and the second chakra.

Orange Zone Power Points Exercise

Find something orange to hold, ideally something from nature, such as a flower, rock, or fruit. As you sit with this orange object for at least five minutes, allow yourself to feel where in your body you resonate to this object. How does the object make you feel emotionally? Try a few different objects, including something man-made, and see how your connection varies. Write about your experience in your Knowing Journal.

The Yellow Zone: The Third Chakra

The third chakra is located in the solar plexus, just above the navel. Our personal "solar power," inner fire or sun, it deals with emotional and personal power issues. Sometimes referred to as the center of the emotions, the yellow chakra governs the spleen, liver, bladder, stomach, and the nervous system. In healing, yellow is associated with education and acquired knowledge, light, will power, mental confusion, intellect, cynicism, indecisiveness, warmth, joy, delight, fear, cowardice, anxiety and nervousness, confusion, depression, solar plexus, liver, nerves, skin, jaundice, and arthritis. The yellow chakra is our social center; feelings of self-acceptance and acceptance from others are dealt with through the third chakra.

Yellow Zone Power Points Exercise

Find something yellow to hold, ideally something from nature such as a flower, leaf, or feather. As you sit with this yellow object for at least five minutes, allow yourself to feel where in your body you resonate to this object. How does the object make you feel emotionally? Try a few different objects, including something man-made, and see how your connection varies. Write about your experience in your Knowing Journal.

The Green Zone: The Fourth Chakra

The heart chakra is located near the heart and is associated with the color green and also pink. Through the green chakra we feel love, compassion, and unconditional acceptance for others (and ourselves). It is the chakra of humanitarian love; emotional love is associated with the third (yellow) chakra. It governs the heart, blood, circulatory system immune system, endocrine system, and thymus gland. In color healing, green is associated with space, the search for truth, growth, nature, fertility, creativity, healing, regeneration, compassion, balance, envy, heart, lungs, thymus, ulcers, and seeing all aspects of a situation. The fourth chakra deals with our need for deep, intimate contact with others as well as the capacity to empathize and sympathize with others. Because this is the "middle" chakra, exactly between the lower three and the upper three, it is the chakra through which the lower physical chakras are connected with the higher, mental/spiritual chakras. For this reason, to me it has always represented the place where the Earthly World meets the Unseen World, particularly in the form of Knowing called mediumship.

Green Zone Power Points Exercise

Find something green to hold, ideally something from nature, such as a new leaf or spice. As you sit with this green object for at least five minutes, allow yourself to feel where in your body you resonate to this object. How does the object make you feel emotionally? Try a few different objects, including something man-made, and see how your connection varies. Write about your experience in your Knowing Journal.

The Blue Zone: The Fifth Chakra

The fifth chakra is located in the throat area and resonates to the color blue. Communication, expression of thoughts and feelings, speaking our personal truth, and judgment are dealt with in this chakra, which is why I consider it the "third ear," where Auditory Intuition is most easily processed. It governs the thyroid gland, lungs, vocal cords, lungs, and metabolism. In color healing, blue is associated with peace, sympathy and healing, rest, divinity, blessing, protection through helpful and supportive influences, intuition, leadership, serenity, calmness, softness, emptiness, feeling blue, frigidity, thyroid, throat, cramps, sprains, infections, and neck problems.

Blue Zone Power Points Exercise

Find something blue to hold, ideally something from nature, such as a crystal, stone, or feather. As you sit with this blue object for at least five minutes, allow yourself to feel where in your body you resonate to this object. How does the object make you feel emotionally? Try a few different objects, including something man-made, and see how your connection varies. Write about your experience in your Knowing Journal.

The Indigo Zone: The Sixth Chakra

The sixth chakra is located in what is called the third eye, at the center of the forehead between the eyebrows. It resonates to the color indigo, a blend of blue and purple that is reminiscent of a midnight blue night sky. It deals with spirituality and the search for meaning in life. Intuition and psychic awareness are stimulated by opening this chakra, as is the imagination. In color healing, it is associated with the face, eyes, ears, nose (sinuses), the central nervous system, and governs the pituitary gland.

Indigo Zone Power Points Exercise

Find something indigo to hold, ideally something from nature such as a flower or feather. Or watch the night sky when it is the midnight blue of indigo. As you sit with the energy of indigo for at least five minutes, allow yourself to feel where in your body you resonate to this vibration. How does the object make you feel emotionally? Try a few different objects, including something man-made, and see how your connection varies. Write about your experience in your Knowing Journal.

The Violet Zone: The Seventh Chakra

The seventh chakra, also known as the crown chakra, is located at the top of the head. This chakra resonates to violet, and is associated also with white and gold. It deals with our connection to the concept higher intelligence, the Universe, God/Goddess and the wisdom and guidance coming from the higher planes. It governs the pineal gland, upper brain, and right eye. In color healing, violet is associated with spirituality, healing, service, contemplation, individualism, awareness and understanding one's life purpose, grief, not wanting to be in the Earthly World, addiction, withdrawal, inner calmness, production of mucus and too much activity.

Violet Zone Power Points Exercise

Find something violet to hold, ideally something from nature such as a flower or crystal. As you sit with this violet object for at least five minutes, allow yourself to feel where in your body you resonate to this object. How does the object make you feel emotionally? Try a few different objects, including something man-made, and see how your connection varies. Write about your experience in your Knowing Journal.

With a basic understanding of the seven major chakras, and how the different chakra colors affect you, you are likely to find that your shorthand color code becomes very efficient. You'll find more information about chakras, and what you can do to enhance them using the elements, music, gemtones, herbs, fragrances, and vocalizations (also called toning) in Appendix E.

✳ ✳ ✳ ✳

If you work with enhancing the colors in your Knowing Self-Portrait, you'll soon notice an increase in embedded signs with many levels of interpretation. You may find that each sign can be interpreted on mental, emotional, spiritual, and physical levels. You'll also notice many signs which represent both a the literal and a symbolic. By becoming more aware of color in the world around you, and the signs that color is showing you, your Knowing will be enhanced.

CHAPTER 18
THE FOUR CORNERS
OF KNOWING

"Trust yourself. You know more than you think you do."
—Benjamin Spock, Baby and Child Care, 1977

Being in that Knowing Zone, where you're almost certain but not quite, where you feel you've onto something but don't want to make a poor decision, can seem overwhelming. You "Know" your best course of action but feel stuck.

That's because generally in our modern society we're not taught to trust our right-brain insight as much as we are our left-brain logic. If we were, we'd feel *and* think our way through life, allowing a blend of both approaches for the best outcomes. But now you are able to approach your intuition systematically using a simple, structured approach I created called the Four Corners of Knowing. As you use it, you'll find that it guides you in the development of an internal compass for your Knowing. You'll feel far less overwhelmed by the array of possibilities, trusting your Knowing Self to guide you, but also checking in with your logical mind.

The Four Corners approach always operates from this moment, Now (just as with everything else in the Earthly World). Used to review your past choices for additional understanding and insight, this simple model can be quite powerful. Carefully considering your past allows you to avoid repeating ineffective patterns by allowing that inner voice, your Knowing Self, to be heard. Considering the past also allows your Knowing Self to gain more understanding of human events. After all, the body-bound you lives here and bears the burden of the journey in this Earthly World. Until, that is, you let your Knowing Self help carry the load.

You can also apply the Four Corners of Knowing to current decisions. By doing so, you'll be at peace, fully aware that you've accessed your Knowing Self and considered the ramifications of your options from several angles. By doing this, no matter how others react or employ their free will, you'll be fine. The fact that we *all* have free will is what complicates things. Free will means that others can change *our* plans through *their* choices, thus messing up those plans and requiring us to make new decisions. But by routinely employing the Four Corners of Knowing in your decision making, you'll allow both your human logic and your inner wisdom to be heard. What more can you ask of yourself than informed, conscious focus on your choices, the stuff of which your life is created? As a result, you'll be better prepared no matter what life tosses at you.

Remember the infinity symbol schematic found in Chapter 1? It's comprised of two loops and looks like an infinity symbol turned so it resembles an 8. The lower loop represents you in the Earthly World, the upper one your Knowing Self in the Unseen World (see page 17). The two loops work together to inform and integrate information from both worlds.

The Four Corners of Knowing Approach is also one of ongoing expansion. Each bit of information fed from earthbound you to your Knowing Self expands the total knowledge base. And each bit of insight you allow to flow in from your Knowing Self also expands the knowledge base. (This suggests that everything you do, every decision you make, has the power to transform the universe, but that's a topic for another book!) The crossing point where the two loops intersect, which I call the Knowing Moment, is also the point of conscious co-creation, the Now. And that's also where the Four Corners of Knowing operate.

Working With the Four Corners of Knowing

The Four Corners of Knowing are Intention, Attention, Reflection, and Evolution. Remember that it is easy to think of the abbreviation I

ARE. It's reminiscent of I AM, which you may be familiar with from the Old Testament Biblical reference, "I am that I am" (Exodus 3:14). I ARE reminds us, although rather ungrammatically, that we are all connected, all one, and that intention is the place things begin. The following diagram shows how you are at the center, Now, in the present moment. Around you are arrayed the Four Corners of Knowing:

The Four Corners of Knowing

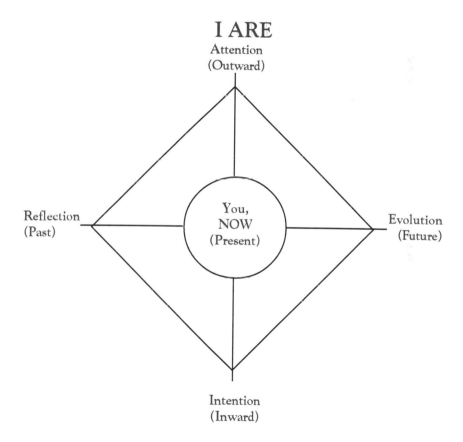

I ARE
Attention
(Outward)

Reflection
(Past)

You,
NOW
(Present)

Evolution
(Future)

Intention
(Inward)

Let's consider the deeper meaning and the key question associated with each of these Four Corners of the I ARE model in turn, beginning with Intention.

I: Intention: The Look Inward

Intention is the place to begin any inquiry to your Knowing Self regarding a decision you are making. Intention is very much an inward process. Whatever it relates to—health, relationships, career, or some other aspect of your life—your intention has a profound, undeniable impact on the outcome. Why? Because your intention establishes the initial vibration you broadcast, and it depends only and entirely on what you choose. It's powerful in ways we don't always understand. Intention addresses the question, What do you want to see?

Where you begin matters immensely in the Intention process. When you come from a place of unselfishness, of positive self-regard and regard for others, your decisions will have an exponential quality, affecting others in positive ways. Think of it as a gong you strike. That resonating tone will carry for a long while, so choosing to strike a harmonious tone rather than a discordant one benefits both you and others.

For many years now, on a regular basis I intend abundance and prosperity for all practitioners in the field of intuition. Every time a wonderful, serendipitous event occurs that helps me take a step forward professionally, I take a moment to appreciate the event. I'm often astounded by the wondrous events which come my way, seemingly without my seeking them. After indulging my "Wow, how great is that! Thank you, Universe" gratitude response, I take a moment to intend on behalf of others. I ask that my good fortune be replicated in some bigger, better way for all who are engaged in similar work with similar intent.

By sharing this positive vibe through my deliberate choice to push it (through intention) into the upper loop of the infinity symbol, and by declaring that others who resonate to it also benefit, I add that positive vibe to the collective energy source we can all draw from. As a result my abundance-for-all intention takes on an exponential quality, and is available to anyone who wants to tap into that vibration. How many wonderful intentions that could benefit you are floating around in the ethers, waiting for you to tune in? Take advantage, take in all that you can. Tune in.

Through intention, my small good fortunes become energized, empowered. Like a snowball rolling down a snowy hill, they grow larger, capable of much larger impact. Try it yourself. It works best—actually it works *only*—when you are completely sincere in your request, un-worried about personal gain or competition, and simply excited that others might partake in the joys you have experienced.

Keep in mind the following:

1. Intention is inward-out. You start the process.
2. Intention becomes exponential as it attracts other intentions which resonate to it.
3. Intention is based on your free will to choose how you wish to view particular aspects of your life.

Do you intend positive outcomes? Then don't let worry or fear trap you. When you feel those emotions, sit with them. Ask your Knowing Self to share insights, signs and support in ways you can understand. Feel the fear, and then take the next step toward your dream.

Intention: A Real-Life Example

My client Joe was going through a very nasty divorce that would affect his business, which had become extremely successful in the four years prior to the breakdown of his 17-year marriage to Susan. He was understandably concerned that the settlement be fair. After all, his success was recent and they'd lived pretty modestly for the first 13 years. Plus, he wasn't yet convinced his business ventures would be successful in the long term. He didn't feel his wife should live what he called a "country club life" in the face of such business uncertainties. Still, Joe offered lifetime alimony as well as a large cash settlement, and the former family home, a significant asset.

But his about-to-be-ex-wife was unwilling to accept what most people (including her attorneys) considered to be a generous settlement offer. For more than two years, the attorney's fees and mediation bills mounted, the tensions increased, and the children, who lived with Joe, suffered emotionally.

When Joe and I met, it was very clear to me through access to his Knowing Self that the solution was a simple one: use the success of his business and the resulting money to change Susan's life, long term. Basically, share the wealth with a bitter, angry ex. Sounds like a roadmap to disaster, doesn't it?

But Joe had already come to understand the principle of intention on his own. My take on the situation strengthened his own Knowing (a role many intuitives serve for their clients). He came up with a plan. He paid for his wife's college education, which had been interrupted when they married at age 20 and started a family shortly thereafter. Joe also decided to make Susan a minority stakeholder in the now successful business, reasoning that her support, focused on the homefront during their marriage, was a form of "sweat equity," and a choice that had limited her career and earning potential. To Joe, it was worth far more than money to allow someone he'd once truly loved, the mother of his four children, to succeed even as he succeeded. (Of course, Joe structured the deal so that her share would be distributed among the children upon her death; he is, after all, a very shrewd businessman.)

Sharing the wealth had other benefits, too, for both Joe and others. His four children, now young adults, would never again listen to their mother's angry protests their father wasn't a good person: How could that be true, given his generosity to her? They witnessed a win-win solution between their divorced parents, in the form of a creative financial partnership. Susan benefited, too: She was able to take a teaching job at a parochial school, a desire of many years, and something she would not have done without the partnership equity payments to make it an affordable option. Perhaps most importantly, with a stake in its success, Susan eventually learned to wish Joe well. She also took an interest in the business, something Joe had spent years during their marriage encouraging.

Wishing her ex-husband well was not an easy lesson for an embittered woman who had previously resented the long hours Joe had spent building a successful company while she cared for four children. But even her grudging good wishes for the success of Joe's business added positive vibes to the pool of possibilities. And Joe's business thrived beyond his previous expectations.

Joe's Knowing Self challenged him to take a remarkable risk, and to his credit, Joe met the challenge by using intention. The resulting payoff was more business than he could have imagined. Recently he's even been able to purchase smaller companies struggling in a tough economy, keeping jobs available to workers who are nearing retirement. The workers' loyalty and gratitude adds even *more* positive energy to that pool of possibilities which Joe now accesses regularly through his Knowing Self. Although he shares a portion of the business profits with Susan, he keeps far more. And the rewards are much more than money.

A: Attention: The Look Outward

The second step of the I ARE model is Attention. Once you've become very clear about your deepest desires, your intention for a particular situation, you can move your focus from inward (what do I really want?) to outward (what would be best for others affected?). Attention addresses the question, What do I want to connect with?

In the Attention step, your goal is to consider how your choice would affect others around you.

Keep in mind the following:

1. Attention is outward. In the Attention step, you observe the process of your unfolding Intention by focusing outward, seeking confirming, and disconfirming signs in the world around you.

2. Attention requires an analytical, thoughtful frame of mind. Observe, record, review, assess. Attention is a very "left brain," focused activity.

3. As Attention focuses your mind, your Intention may change. Attention to details and signs may cause you to reframe your intention as you gather more data and build a more complete picture. In other words, focusing on what benefits others may change your Intention.

Do you pay attention to the signs that come your way regularly? Do you notice synchronicities and odd little patterns? If not, you may need to ask yourself where you are placing your Attention.

Attention: A Real-Life Example of Seeking Signs

Katherine worked her way up from an entry-level position at a Fortune 100 company to a management role in which she was responsible for the workings of three departments and a staff of over 40. Even with all her successes and her genuine fondness for her job and the organization, it felt incomplete. The reason?

Years ago, Katherine had formed an intention to own a business of her own someday. But she'd never taken the time to focus her attention on exactly what sort of business would bring her both financial support and personal fulfillment. Finally she decided that paying attention to the signs around her might lead her in the right direction. She decided to look outward for clues.

"I was quite aware that 14 years in a corporate environment was long enough for me, even though I was good at my job and, for the most part, liked it. But when I turned 38, I decided that by the time I was 40, I wanted to make my business dream come true," Katherine said. "But I had no idea whether I should buy a franchise of some sort, or build my own thing.

"So I started to watch other people and talk to them about their work. At parties, conferences, and events I started to pay attention to what got people excited. When they talked about something they loved, you could feel it, at least I could, like butterflies in my stomach, just a little queasiness. After realizing it was partly a clue to what got me excited, I decided to really pay attention to my stomach's signals," she continued.

"For about 2 months I noticed that it was writing and communications that got the most positive reaction from my stomach. I also noticed during that period that I was being offered many chances to travel with friends and for work. It was weird, it seemed everyone was traveling and saying, 'you should come, too.' At work new assignments sent me out with the sales staff on a pretty regular basis, too, although usually as a purchasing manager, I'm on the inside. Soon I realized that when I couldn't take all the travel opportunities, I felt a great deal of disappointment. By paying attention to the signs around me, through my body and my emotions, it dawned on me: I needed to somehow combine writing and travel. So I took an intensive course in travel writing, and I've been making a pretty comfortable living at it for 3 years now. This year I'll make about three-quarters of what I did before, but my quality of life is at least 10 times better. And soon I'll surpass my old earnings level."

The step of Attention served Katherine well. She'd had a sense of her direction for years: a business of her own. But it was through looking outward to what brought joy to others that she was exposed to ideas that moved her closer to her heart's desire, a desire she'd not even known was there. She also paid attention to synchronicities, which led her to the path that she was near—but not quite on—for many years.

R: Reflection: The Look Backward

The third step of the I ARE model is Reflection. Once you've clarified your Intention and fine-tuned your plans through Attention, reflecting on your life to see what, from the past, might block your progress is time well spent. Although living entirely focused on the past is unwise, reflection helps us to look for insights and lessons in our unique life experiences. This helps us to make choices from a more balanced, wise perspective. The goal of the Reflection step is to consider how your past experiences and choices influence you now, and particularly whether they cloud your view or block your progress in any way. Reflection addresses the question, What do I want to release?

Keep in mind the following:

1. Reflection is focused on the past. You live in the Now and the past is always...well...passed. It can never happen again in exactly that way again. So relax: it will never be like that again, no matter what "it" was like.

2. Reflection requires a willingness to feel old wounds, hurts, and unfinished business in order to assess its current impact. Looking for repeated patterns is key; those are the places to dig a bit deeper for insight. Reflection, like Intention, is about going inward for answers.

3. Reflection benefits from allowing full expression to your feelings. While the Knowing Journal asks you to observe data, you can also create a section in it to record your reflections on the past and what you've learned. You may surprise yourself.

Reflection: Healing the Past

Like many people, Matt had experienced sexual abuse as a child. The molestation had occurred on three or four occasions one summer at camp, when he was 11 years old. Matt had always felt that his abuse had shaped him into a less trusting person than he hoped to be, particularly in relationships with women.

> *"But I didn't understand why being with women in a committed, romantic relationship was so difficult for me," Matt said. "After all, my abuser was a guy, five years older than me. It only happened a few times. It was over 20 years ago. So it didn't make sense. But I decided to take a long, hard look at my life. I'm 32 now and I've been engaged twice, but broke both of them off, and needed to know what was going on with me.*

> "Working with my therapist, I reflected on the past. I realized I'd skated right past the feelings that being molested had left me with. I told myself, then and for almost 20 years after, that it amounted to a few hours of my life and I shouldn't let it affect me. I just didn't let myself feel the fear, the anger, the shame, the absolute fury of being manipulated and taken advantage of in that way. All that stuff was really blocking my progress in relationships.

> "It was very difficult to go back to that summer and really deeply feel the experience on an emotional level. Having someone walk with me on this road, my therapist, made it feel much safer. Still, I never would have suspected that a few hours of my life could have blocked me in relationships for 20 years, but that's what I found out. Clearing that up is the best investment of time I ever made. The process of reflection, of really feeling the original stress and pain, changed my life. I feel lighter. Fears that developed because of that summer, which I didn't even know I had, were taken away. Now there's much more room for joy. And I'm seeing that as I make new friendships," Matt said. "Reflecting on painful times and having the courage to go there again with fresh eyes changed everything."

Whether you experienced sexual or physical abuse, bullying by other children at school, critical comments by adults, mean remarks by a lover, sibling, teacher, friend, or spouse, you've experienced wounds that may be festering. And limiting your life if you diminish the pain associated with them.

Like Matt, your linear, logical left brain may try to minimize the impact of fear, shame or anger, which is understandable. We all want to push pain away; it hurts. But through the step of Reflection you can learn to meet and clear the blocks in your life. The freeing power of releasing old wounds will help you move forward to the next step of the I ARE model: Evolution.

E: Evolution: The Look Forward

The last step of the I ARE model is Evolution. It's focused on what you would like to unfold or evolve. Yes, we can only ever live Now, but we still need some sense of direction in our lives. Taking the step of

Evolution is similar to planning a road trip: you look at the destination you're headed for, and decide the best way to get there. You'll also have to consider the possibility of detours, changes in plans made by your or others, and construction delays. In some ways, Evolution is the flowering of Intention. That's because Intention is Now, it's the first vibration, that rich tone as the gong is struck. Evolution is like the last hovering note you hear, softly. It's the completion of a process, off in the future, but already set in motion. It addresses the question, What do you want to be?

One woman who asked—and answered—this important question was Althea, an African American who'd grown up in rural Georgia. Overall she was pleased with her life, but considering what she really wanted to do rather late in life still changed everything for her.

"I've lived a good life. I'm 66 now," Althea said. "Healthy. Happy. Blessed, really. But I have always wanted to be a painter. My daughter and two sons knew that. We'd never had money when I was growing up, or when my kids were kids. I never made it beyond high school, although I wanted to. And in those days, art wasn't in the curriculum. I couldn't afford art lessons, especially after my husband died 17 years ago. I painted with the kids when they were small, worked with crafts, fixed up the house, and painted when I could, just for myself. I was raising a family and working. So my dream to be a painter never really came together. I really didn't pursue it."

"But I was fine with that, I really was. Or at least, that's what I thought. Then for my 60th birthday my kids all got together and bought me six months worth of weekly private lessons with a well-known local artist. I have never had such fun, never felt so right about anything, even being a mother, which I also love. But painting is truly what I was meant to do; it's why God put me here," Althea said.

"I have no bitterness about not getting around to painting until my 60s. My art is better in some ways because I had a different life before this. Many artists I know are not passionate about their work after 30 years; that's understandable. Me—I'm excited! I paint for 5 or 6 hours almost every day; it never feels like work. People are buying my paintings. I even have a show coming up in the fall," Althea said. "And

*next year, I'm going to Italy to paint for three weeks. My kids
are coming, too, with their families. We're renting a place
together. My life has evolved into something I could never
have imagined. I feel complete."*

Althea always held her dream, although quietly. She didn't actively
put her intention "out there." But she was able to evolve into an artist
at a time in life when many people are slowing down, largely because
she'd pursued her interests in art, even if in small ways, and shared her
sense of her life's purpose with her children. They knew how much
painting meant to Althea, and found a way to help her evolve into the
artist she is, and always was.

The final step of Evolution feels inevitable, as if we could do nothing else, as Althea demonstrates. Even if you aren't sure yet where your
Evolution will take you, by working with Intention, Attention, and
Reflection, you'll begin to see signs of the place you are meant to go, of
your life purpose and destiny unfolding gently before you. Then you
can address the question of what are you meant to be, the most future-
focused question of the Four Corners of Knowing model. In that process you're likely to find that you can pull yourself back to this moment,
Now, feeling completely at ease about where life is taking you.

Why?

Because you'll Know it's absolutely right.

The Four Key Questions

The Four Corners of Knowing, are easily remembered by the letters
I-A-R-E reminding us that all creation and life change begins with I or
Intention. Here are the four key questions that The Four Corners of
Knowing brings to you for consideration:

1. Intention: What do you want to see?
2. Attention: With what do you want to connect?
3. Reflection: What do you want to release?
4. Evolution: What do you want to be?

Consider these four corners through the power of your own Knowing
and transform your life. Once you do that, living in the Knowing Zone
will become a natural outcome of your inward journey to understand
your natural-born intuitive style, your values, and your Knowing Self.

CHAPTER 19
LIVING IN THE KNOWING ZONE

"Any life, no matter how long and complex it may be, is made up of a single moment—the moment in which a man finds out, once and for all, who he is."

—Jorge Luis Borges

Living in that Knowing Zone—the place where ideas and insights flow endlessly and powerfully, where reason and logic support and enhance your intuitive awareness, where it all seems to come together—is a natural outgrowth of the process of delving inward. Learning to sit with your Knowing Self, to take quiet time to hear what's not said in words, see what's not shown in pictures, and feel what only the heart knows is an important step on the road to Knowing. Only through the thoughtful inward journey can your Knowing be developed into shorthand signs and symbols that guide you through life. When you've figured out how to tap into the Knowing Zone by using the ideas in this book, and perhaps even taken them a step further by allowing your intuition to lead you into personalized techniques that fit you perfectly, the next goal is to learn to live from the Knowing Zone.

Regular use of the Four Corners of Knowing will help you develop a way of working out decisions using both your intuitive right brain and your logical left brain. You're also likely to find that you internalize the

I ARE framework through regular use. You'll no longer need to move through it step by step. Instead, you'll find you process all Four Corners of Knowing almost simultaneously. You're also likely to find that one of the four corners seems most comfortable. Use that corner as a starting point, but don't forget to look at all four corners of Knowing: Intention, Attention, Reflection, and Evolution.

When people learn to live from this centered, constantly available source of inner wisdom, they find their lives are transformed. They find themselves in circumstances better than they might have imagined all because they took the time to blend an inward journey with their own inner wisdom and analyze the information and experiences life brings. Here are some stories of how living in the Knowing Zone changed lives for the better in big ways.

Susan's Story: My Perfect Home

Coming out of a divorce, Susan, age 53, was faced with many tough decisions. One was where to live. A freelance writer with two adult children off living lives of their own, she was fortunate to have no restrictions on the possibilities; her life was very flexible. But fear still paralyzed her.

> *"I didn't want to make a mistake in choosing to live out what I expect to be one of the most interesting times of my life in a place I don't like. I also felt I didn't have time to live for a year each in two or three places to see what fit best," Susan said. "I wasn't afraid of moving, but I was afraid of making a wrong choice at this stage of life."*

Every choice we make teaches us something important if we're willing to examine it. There are no wrong choices, only learning journeys. But like most of us, Susan sought to reduce discomfort and increase joy through her decision about where to live; she wanted to keep this learning curve to the minimum. So she approached the task of where to live like the investigative journalist she'd once been.

> *"I delved right into the fact-finding, mostly online," Susan said. "I looked up everything from weather patterns to income levels to real estate appreciation. And health care options and car insurance rates and even what the local grocery stores were like. I found a few websites that helped me along the*

way. But even with all this really useful information, I felt very disconnected from all the places I liked. None of the places felt like home.

"I was fine with renting an apartment for a year after the divorce from James, but now it was time to sign another lease. That didn't feel right either. I decided to try what had been suggested to me before: go within and see, trust my own sense of Knowing."

Very strong in both Sensory Intuition and Visual Intuition, Susan was struggling. She trusted her Knowing Self to provide some insights.

"I did some journaling, some inner exploration. I thought about all the places I'd traveled in the world. I paid attention to which ones I had the best memories about. I even went through boxes of old vacation photos to bring myself right back to the moment, to make sure I was right about which ones had the best memories! I'll admit it, I was getting a little compulsive, but I didn't want to make a mistake. At 53, I felt I wanted to find the perfect place to spend the next 30 or 40 years. Or at least 20!

"And even with all that data I collected, the place I felt best about wasn't on the short list. It was through looking at photos of a family trip we took about 25 years ago that I found my perfect place. James and I were on our way to Florida with our children, and we detoured through a town in Virginia, on the Chesapeake Bay. We had an absolutely perfect day there; we liked it so much we stayed over. One of the most perfect days of my life and I'd completely forgotten. But when I found that picture, I just Knew I would move there; I felt it in my heart, I really did. Of course that seemed silly, so I decided to do my left-brain analysis. Back online I went, back to the investigation," Susan said.

"My friend Maria came with me for a vacation there. And I found it. My place in Virginia. A small house in a small town on the bay. I've lived here three years now, and feel like my soul is at rest. I write better here. I live better here. I even have a love here, my friend Raymond, who's taught me to sail. I trusted my inner wisdom and am so glad I did it

thoughtfully. Because otherwise, I would have settled for 'just anyplace' with good weather and nice people. Instead, I found my place," Susan said. "I knew I would."

Susan has learned to live from her Knowing Zone. By using both her right brain's insights based on feelings and memories, and adding her left brain's logical analysis, she managed to find a life even better than she ever imagined. The journey to her own Knowing helped her find inner peace. You too can learn to live from this place. The road to Knowing Zone starts with Intention.

Mark's Story: The Right Work at Midlife

At 41, Mark was happily married to Cynthia, his wife of 15 years. Together they had three children: Josh, age 11; Celia, age 9; and Marcie, age 6. An operations manager for a utility company for 20 years, Mark had built a comfortable life with his family in the suburbs of a good-sized Midwestern city. When the company chose to automate many of the processes he'd been overseeing, Mark was offered the opportunity to accept a fairly generous buyout offer. It included enough money to give him a year to explore and plan a way to retrain in a new career.

"Even with the buyout, we were terrified of what was going to happen to us," Mark recalled. "Would we lose the house, would there be enough money for the kids to go on to college. Josh was already 11; now he's 15 so the time's coming soon. Would Cynthia—she's a registered nurse—have to go from part-time work to full-time? All those questions.

"We figured we'd work it out somehow, and decided to take the first few weeks after I lost my job to just relax. It was such a stressful time that as I look back on it, it was the smartest move I ever made. Because in that time, I found myself really thinking about what would make me happy work-wise. I had never done that before, really. I chose my college major, engineering, because that's what my aptitude tests suggested I'd be good at. And I was. I graduated near the top of my class, and because I was already working at the plant during college—I had to work my way through—it was easy to fall right into the job," Mark said.

We've all done it: let the path of least resistance carry us along. Mark was lucky, though, to realize he'd been handed the gift of a lifetime: a job loss, and a chance to change his life's work.

"I have a family and that's the best thing, the most rewarding thing I am involved with. So I had never deeply considered what I really wanted to do for work until this job elimination. With a family to take care of, I thought my options were limited. But with Cynthia's support and feedback, I took the time to look at my life and uncover my dreams.

"I realized after really thinking about the jobs I'd held, and what I liked about my work that it's training others that really makes me happy. But the truth is being a dad is my favorite job. It really is. But they don't pay you for that one," Mark said. *"And owning a daycare center is not for me, but we did consider it. I'm not cut out for the entrepreneurial thing. I don't want to own the company."*

Mark was wise to trust his own Knowing, and solicit the feedback of his wife Cynthia, whom he's known since he was 24 years old. He also took the time to consider what fits his interests; he knows he doesn't want the complete responsibility of running a company. Together with Cynthia, Mark devised a family plan to get them through this tough time.

"My kids were scared. There I was, 41, out of work and thinking about retraining in a new career. Of course they were panicked; I was too. But I Knew this was my chance. I Knew it. I just felt it in my gut," Mark said. *"So I took advantage of the outplacement counseling, and eventually decided to go for a master's degree in teaching after a lot of soul-searching. Was I too old? Could we afford it? Should I choose training and consulting where there'd be more money, but also lots of trave? All that stuff,"* Mark said.

"Teaching just felt right. It took two years, and Cynthia had to go to work full time, but it's worked out better than we'd imagined. I'm not on call 24/7 anymore so the stress levels are better. I'm a nicer guy. I make less money teaching at the vocational program in engineering technologies, but it turns out Cynthia loves working full time, so we're okay.

We're careful, the kids know that shooting for scholarships is
more important now, so they're really focused on the aca-
demics," Mark said.

Besides the changes in his work life, Mark found that finding his
passion, the work that brings him the greatest ability to be fully present
in the Now, rather than stressed about the future, paid off in other
ways, too. His family life is enriched.

"The time with the kids after school has changed my relationships with them; I was a good dad before but now, I'm a
fantastic dad," Mark said, smiling. "I mean it: being a great
dad, that's my 'thing,' what I was meant to do.

"And I cook more, too. Now I'm thinking about taking
some classes in that; Cynthia's going to join me. We're talking about a family vacation in Europe next summer, in the
countryside somewhere. We'll rent a place where we can cook.
Have a chef out to show us how to cook the local specialties.
That'll cost less than a restaurant meal for five. And the
memories, that's the thing. We Know the memories we're
making are priceless. Losing my job four years ago was the
best thing that ever happened to me. I never thought I'd say
that," Mark said. "But I Know it's true."

Like Susan, Mark has learned to live from the Knowing Zone. By
taking the time to pay attention to the signs of opportunities buried in
a job loss, by reflecting for the first time on the question of what he
wanted to release, Mark was able to answer the question, *What do I
want to be?* For him the answer is a father first, a teacher second and
maybe a chef, third.

Megan's Story: The Right Relationship

Megan felt that her life required some reflection and review, particularly about romantic relationships. Now age 31, she'd been engaged
once, at age 26, but broke it off just seven weeks before the wedding.
Family and friends, and Megan herself, still spoke highly of Jeff, her ex.
But in her heart of hearts, Megan knew that Jeff had not been the best
match for her. She'd attended his wedding just a year earlier, truly happy
to see him marry a woman for whom he really was a terrific match.

"When I saw Jeff and Kara together, I Knew it was right for them in a way it never was for us. I'm really glad for them both; they're good people. And it was a little sad in a way, because it's almost five years ago now that we broke it off, and in that time, I've only had three relationships. The longest was for seven months. I've been feeling like I just don't have whatever it takes to be in a long-term relationship or be married," Megan said.

But Megan is self-aware and has a good self-understanding. She's very clear in her ability to assess herself. She took the time for an inward journey as a step toward Knowing what's best for her in her life.

"I don't feel as though I'm a loser or anything. I'm successful, educated, and have lots of friends. But I've had to really consider what it is about me, about my interactions with men in whom I'm interested, that's behind this. Is it me? Is it karma? I finally had to look into that," Megan said. "And I got some answers that changed anything."

Megan explained that she spent several weeks keeping a record of her interactions with people, both men and women, and how her body reacted to them. She also tracked her dreams.

"I learned that there's a particular reaction I am prone to with certain people that tells me I'm in what I call my 'safety zone.' My body relaxes and I feel quite comfortable. It's a nice, safe feeling. But by looking forward using the evolution step, I determined that a comfortable relationship in the safety zone is not in my best interests," Megan said. "I need something that challenges me, that makes me feel stretched, excited, vibrant. And I also learned that this discovery meant that I'd have to be the one to put myself out there. This information came mostly through my dreams, which had themes about standing alone and reaching back, above, or across to others. I finally figured out that every relationship I've had, going back to my first high school boyfriend, was one in which I reacted. They chose me, not the other way around," Megan said. "Figuring that out was huge for me. It changed everything."

Megan then explained with much laughter that she spent the next several months reaching out to datable men in a variety of situations.

> "I decided it was time for me to choose what I wanted. I
> tried online dating services, speed dating, friend set-ups—
> you name it, I tried it. I could write a book (maybe I should).
> What an adventure. My goal in those four months wasn't to
> meet a man exactly, but to learn to reach past my comfort
> zone. And that's when I met a man with whom I can foresee
> a future—Zachary," Megan said.

Megan met Zachary in the most ordinary of ways: while out with
friends.

> "I was with a girlfriend and two couples. We were wait-
> ing for about 45 minutes for our seats at a favorite restaurant
> one Friday night after work. We weren't the only ones doing
> so. Zachary was there with some buddies after work. He's
> four years younger than me. That was a risk for me," Megan
> joked. "But we really click; we're talking about getting mar-
> ried next year. He makes me feel a little unsafe. Not scared,
> or uneasy, but like I know he's changing, and that means
> our relationship will also always be changing. That's exciting.
> That's what I Know will work for me. A man who won't
> stagnate," Megan said. "Because I'll never stagnate. That I
> Know."

Megan, like Susan and Mark, was willing to take the inward journey to her own Knowing, and to trust her intuition as well as analyze
the patterns of her choices to gain insight. By discerning what her Knowing Self was trying to convey to her, Megan has found the most excit-
ing, rewarding, and challenging romance in which she's ever been
involved.

What About You?

What would you like from your life?

Do you Know?

Would you like to?

By now, I hope you Know that you can find this out.

It takes is a willingness to trust your natural-born intuition, your
inner wisdom, your Knowing Self. It takes a willingness to explore
your natural-born intuition, to delve inward to uncover your natural

intuitive style. It takes a working understanding of the forces that drive you, your values, which underlie all your choices in life. It requires an ongoing commitment to working with the Four Corners of Knowing: Intention, Attention, Reflection, and Evolution. It requires asking—and even better, answering—four simple questions.

Intention: What do you want to see?

Attention: With what do you want to connect?

Reflection: What do you want to release?

Evolution: What do you want to be?

I'm glad to have served as a guide thus far, pointing you in the direction of your own Knowing. And I'm honored that you've taken the time to explore your inner landscape, discern what makes you uniquely you—your intuitive style, your values, your life experiences, your choices. What you want to see, to connect with, to release. To be.

Through continued systematic observation, you can learn to attune yourself to your Knowing Self. And from there, to learn to enter and live in the Knowing Zone. And from there, to the most powerful place of all: the place where the worlds connect, where right brain meets left brain, where logic meets sensation, where thought meets feeling, where your inner wisdom becomes your trusted friend and wise adviser. This is the place where your Knowing Self comes together with knowledge of the world to guide you gently along this journey.

Are you ready for the adventure?

I asked this question of you earlier. I hope your answer is still yes because the journey into your own Knowing, to meet and work with your Knowing Self is not over. It's never over. It's an ongoing process, like the rest of life. An ongoing adventure.

I hope you'll decide to continue the adventure we've begun together, to Know more, to take the journey inward. If you do, I promise you one simple thing:

More from your life.

YOUR KNOWING SELF–PORTRAIT

How Your Intuitive Style Aligns with Your Values (by Color)

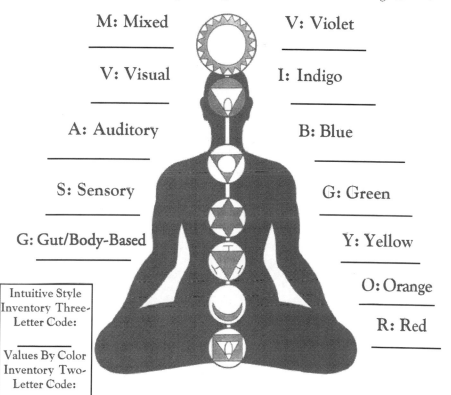

M: Mixed
_____

V: Visual
_____

A: Auditory
_____

S: Sensory
_____

G: Gut/Body-Based
_____

V: Violet
_____

I: Indigo
_____

B: Blue
_____

G: Green
_____

Y: Yellow
_____

O: Orange

R: Red
_____

Intuitive Style
Inventory Three-
Letter Code:

Values By Color
Inventory Two-
Letter Code:

_____

APPENDIX B
KEEPING A KNOWING JOURNAL

Adapt these suggestions for keeping a Knowing Journal to fit your style and goals. After all, it's yours—do it your way.

Your Knowing Self is always ready to assist you. The major key access your Knowing Self is the Knowing Journal. Remember that your Knowing Journal is not a diary. A Journal is about your inner being; a diary is about the world around you. Your Knowing Journal is a self-improvement tool, not simply a record of events.

Your Knowing Journal allows you to monitor your internal processes. It helps you to integrate inner conflicts, to bring things to the surface for healing. Your Knowing Journal also shows the changing cycles within your life, processes that only become evident under rigorous self-examination. It helps you to remember your dreams, to begin to understand and gain insight from them. Most importantly, your Knowing Journal leads you to closer connection with your Knowing Self, that part of you responsible for creativity and inner wisdom, guiding you toward the highest and best from your life. Keeping a Knowing Journal moves you from a seemingly random succession of events into an observer and interpreter of the interaction between the Unseen World and the Earthly World. You begin to see the lessons in your life and put them into practice.

First, choose a suitable Journal. An 8 1/2 x 11 notebook with either lined or unlined paper will work fine. Section dividers are very helpful. Avoid a structured calendar. If you prefer, use a file folder, some loose sheets of paper, and a set of dividers for filing in sections. A computer file or blog will do, but most people find that the process of literally putting pen to paper opens up their creativity and insight even more.

Section One: Daily Log

Make brief entries throughout the day, immediately after events. Record any internal events that you deem important. Emotions, reactions, thoughts, realizations, interactions with people or situations, and the internal effects they had upon you. If there was an external trigger, record just enough of it to make sense of the entry. Brevity is the goal; you want enough data to analyze patterns, not so much to become mired in it.

Even though your outer life may be relatively uneventful from one day to the next, you will soon find that your inner life is alive and rich with eventful happenings. Over time your Knowing Self will bring you even more insights. For instance, you will begin to perceive the triggers that cause your reactions. You will become increasingly aware of how you handle yourself and how you could do better. You will become less "automatic" and more conscious of your choices in every situation.

Section Two: Dream Journal

Record *any* impressions, fragments, or complete dreams that you recall. If you don't normally remember your dreams, keep your Knowing Journal by your bed and record anything that you remember. Tell yourself before you sleep that you *will* remember your dreams. Some people like to use a tape or digital recorder, and later record their dreams in writing, prompted by the short phrases on the tape. If you still don't remember anything, consider setting an alarm clock to waken you at some point in the night; between 2 and 4 a.m. is generally a very active dream time. Write down whatever you recall as soon as you wake. If the answer is nothing, reset the alarm clock.

Section Three: Insight Requests

These can relate to any area of your life: relationships, spirituality, work, creativity, and so on. You are asking your Knowing Self to guide you toward the answers.

Write your entry here in the form of a question, date it, and leave it. Then pay attention to your dreams, the events of the day, your own insights, and synchronicities. Then review the other parts of your Knowing Journal, which fit beautifully together to give you the answers you seek. Intend an answer; eventually it will come. If nothing happens, simply repeat the process the next day with the same question. Be persistent.

Section Four: Transitions and Events

Reflect on your life and recognize the major transitions and events. Witness the cycles of change in your life. Consider and evaluate the various changes you've grown through. Pay attention to the cycles, the ebbs and flows in your marriage or partnership, in long-standing friendships, in your leisure pursuits, even in the places you like to visit or long to live. Write the main events that made it up as a series of brief entries. If you do this properly, you should also be able to identify minor cycles within the major ones. Do this also for the current cycle in which you are living right now.

Suggested Format for Interpreting Signs in Dreams and Synchronicities

The following chart is an example of how you might interpret signs and symbols. For example, if you'd jotted down a request for insight about your marriage in Section Three of your Knowing Journal, you might record information as shown. The last entry, what the pattern suggests, will provide you with perspective to help you make better choices. And of course, use the I ARE model of Intention, Attention, Reflection, and Evolution to flesh it out further before making life-changing decisions.

Sign and Date	Type	Links
Truck, wedding cake March 1	Visual, external, natural world	Birds, nature, wedding.
Song, *Wind Beneath My Wings* March 3	Auditory, external, manmade world	My wedding: this was the song we first danced to as a married couple.
Feeling of Grandma Martha March 4	Very strong "felt sense" of her, as I remember her...like she was in the room	Her anniversary was March 4; I associate to my own wedding and anniversary, the 53-year marriage my grandparents had.
What the pattern suggests:	That I should take a closer look at my marriage and work at that relationship for a while before making a decision about moving on.	

A Final, Important Point

Your Knowing Journal is private. It's meant to be a place where you can say what you wish openly. Don't edit or censor yourself. Carefully choose those with whom to share it, if anyone. Use your Knowing Journal as a safe space, the one place where you can speak freely. So give yourself that freedom, that access to your own Knowing.

APPENDIX C
RECLAIMING YOUR PASSION
AND PURPOSE

To help you connect with your passion and purpose in life, of which your Knowing Self is aware but which may be so buried underneath the layers of life experiences you've built over the years, complete the following statements that draw on different aspects of your intuitive knowing. Record your responses and reactions in your Knowing Journal.

Visual Intuition

Complete the following sentences with a few words, or as much detail as you like:

* When I see a nature scene that I'm particularly moved by, I _____.
* The art, sculpture, and decorations in my home are _____.
* If I had to spend a week doing something with my hands, it would be _____.
* When I'm stressed out, I handle my frustrations by _____.
* The most beautiful thing I've ever seen is _____.

Auditory Intuition

Complete the following sentences with a few words, or as much detail as you like:

* When I hear music I'm particularly moved by, I
  _____.

* The sounds that matter most to me, that I'd most miss if I never heard them again, are _____.

* When I hear the sound of a bell, it reminds me of
  _____.

* When I hear the sound of children laughing, it reminds me of _____.

* When I hear the sounds of birds chirping, I feel
  _____.

* When I hear the sounds of sacred music from the tradition in which I was raised, or chose later, I feel
  _____.

Sensory Intuition

Complete the following sentences with a few words, or as much detail as you like:

* When I taste food that I particularly enjoy, I
  _____.

* The sensations that matter most to me, that I'd most miss if I never felt them again, are _____.

* When I feel the touch of a person I love, it reminds me of _____.

* When I'm afraid, my body tells me through _____.

* When I hold a pet, it reminds me of _____.

* When I hold a child, I _____.

Now, review the previous statements, paying attention not only to the words you used, but also to how you felt emotionally and physically as you responded. Did any of the statements make you feel as if you'd like to keep writing? Were there any on which you simply "blanked"? Which one is your favorite answer?

These emotional responses are part of the database you'll need to completely understand your way of Knowing, so jot it down in your Knowing Journal, or make a voice recording.

Appendix D

Tips for Simplifying and Integrating Meditation

Here are some simple ways to add meditation to your life in small "bites." Now there are no excuses for not taking quiet time for your Knowing Self to gain access to you and help you transform your life.

* Before getting out of bed in the morning, roll up a towel and place it behind your head to give your neck a gentle stretch for five to 10 minutes. While you let your neck stretch, focus on your breathing, following it in and out.

* At your workplace on a lunch or other break, turn off all phones. Dim the lights. Sit quietly in a chair with your back straight, or, if you prefer, with your back against the wall.

* While cooking, turn off all electronic devices including phones, televisions, and CD players. If possible, keep other people out of your kitchen. Just focus on the preparation of the food for five to 10 minutes, thinking only of the food. This can be done with any other rather routine task involving your hands, such as gardening or folding laundry.

APPENDIX E
AURA COLOR
INTERPRETATIONS

Pages 208-210 provide charts to help you enhance or extend your natural intuitive style through color, sound, and by focusing on particular body parts.

Chakra	Root	Spleen	Solar Plexus	Heart	Throat	Third Eye/Ear	Crown
Sanskrit Name	Muladhara	Svadhisthana	Manipura	Anahata	Visudda	Ajna	Sahasrara
Location	Base of Spine	Below Navel	Above Navel	Center of Chest	Throat	Center of Forehead	Top of Head
Color	Red	Orange	Yellow	Green or Pink	Blue	Indigo	Violet
Element	Earth	Water	Fire	Air	Ether	Light	Thought
Musical Note	Middle C	D	E	F	G	A	B
Vocalization	"ooh"	"o" as in "home"	"o" as in "top"	"ah"	"eh"	"ee"	"ohm"
Gland	Adrenal	Reproductive Hormones	Pancreas	Thymus	Thyroid	Pituitary	Pineal
Body Parts	body solids bones, teeth, nails, blood, cellular regeneration, colon, rectum	reproductive organs, kidneys, bladder	liver, spleen, gallbladder, nervous system, lower back	heart, circulation, lower lungs, skin, immune system, upper back, ribs	jaw, neck, throat, voice, air passages, upper lungs, arms	endocrine system, left-brain hemisphere, left eye, nose, ears, sinuses, peripheral nervous system	cerebrum, right-brain hemisphere, right eye, central nervous system

Chakra	Root	Spleen Spleen	Solar Plexus	Heart	Throat	Third Eye/Ear	Crown
Gemstones	Agate, Bloodstone, Hematite, Red Coral, Red Garnet, Ruby	Carnelian, Coral, Gold Calcite, Moonstone	Amber, Citrine, Tiger's Eye, Topaz, Yellow Sapphire	Emerald, Green Jade, Kunzite, Rose Quartz, Tourmaline	Aquamarine, Blue Sapphire, Chalcedony, Turquoise	Azurite, Calcite, Lapis Lazuli, Sodalite, Quartz	Alexandrite, Amethyst, Clear Quartz, Diamond, Selenite
Herbs	Cedar, Clove, Pepper	Gardenia, Sandalwood, Ylang-Ylang	Bergamot, Carnation, Lavender, Rosemary	Marjoram, Geranium, Jasmine, Lavender, Rose oil, Yarrow	Basil, Chamomile, Cypress, Eucalyptus, Frankincense, Sage	Jasmine, Mint, Star Anise	Frankincense, Lotus, Neroli, Rose, Spruce
Essential Oils & Fragrances	Balsam de Peru, Myrrh, Patchouli, Rosewood, Thyme, Vetiver	Benzoin, Cardamon, Clary Sage, Eleni, Fennel, Sandalwood	Bergamot, Black Pepper, Cardamom, Cedarwood, Coriander, Hyssop, Juniper, Lime, Lavender, Rosemary	Marjoram, Geranium, Jasmine, Lavender, Mandarin, Melissa, Rose, Tangerine, Ylang-Ylang	Benzoin, Basil, Chamomile, Cypress, Eucalyptus, Frankincense, Hyssop, linden blossom, Peppermint, Rosewood, Sage	Anise, Angelica seed, Hyacinth, Jasmine, Juniper, Lemon, Pine	Frankincense, Neroli, Rose, Pine

Chakra	Root	Spleen	Solar Plexus	Heart	Throat	Third Eye/Ear	Crown
Qualities & Functions	Survival, power, vitality, grounding, material security, stillness, courage, stability	Primal feelings, awe, enthusiasm, openness to others, personal creativity	Personal power, social identity, influence, authority, self-control, energy, will, peace, radiance, joy, inner harmony, vitality, inner strength	Unconditional love, harmony, forgiveness, healing, compassion, understanding, personal transformation, warmth, sharing, devotion, selflessness	Creative self-expression, communications, inspiration, wisdom, confidence, integrity, truth, freedom, independence	Inner vision, intuition, clairvoyance, perception, insight, imagination, peace of mind, concentration, projection of will, manifestation	Perfection, integration, understanding, divine, unity, wisdom, purpose, universal consciousness, enlightenment
I statement	I have	I feel	I can	I love	I speak	I see	I know

Appendix I
The Meanings of Aura Colors and Numbers

Use this information to help you interpret dreams, messages, and symbols from your Knowing Self.

Brief Interpretations of Numbers 1 to 9

Number	Key Words
1	Initiating action, pioneering, leading, independent, attaining, individual.
2	Cooperation, adaptability, consideration of others, partnering, mediating.
3	Expression, verbalization, socialization, the arts, the joy of living.
4	A foundation, order, service, struggle against limits, steady growth.
5	Expansiveness, visionary, adventure, the constructive use of freedom.
6	Responsibility, protection, nurturing, community, balance, sympathy.
7	Analysis, understanding, knowledge, awareness, studious, meditating.
8	Practical endeavors, status oriented, power-seeking, material goals.
9	Humanitarian, giving nature, selflessness, obligations, creative expression.

Brief Interpretations of Chakra Colors

Color   Key Words

Red   Materialistic thoughts, thoughts about the physical body. Predominantly red aura indicates a materialistically oriented person.

Orange Sensitivity, claisentience, compassion, vicitm, healing for self and others, uncertainty, impressionable, balancing ot harmonizing, naive. Orange relates to the adrenal glands.

Yellow Person power, controlling, opposed to change, scientific, analytical or intellectual, judgemental, self starter, independaent, perfectionist, stubborn, worry or anxiety, secretive, ingenuity and mental agility. Yellow relates to the spleen and life force energy.

Green Renewal, growth or change, näivete, attracting energy, physical discomfort, abundance, deception, neutralizing or calming, affinity or healing distrust or doubt, future time energy. Green relates to thymus and the immune system.

Blue   Communication, inner voice, certainty, integrity, creativity, conscience, melancholy, male energy, clarity, faith and trust, spiritual arrogance, immaturity, cold personality, emotional health, learning obsessive. Blue relates to thyroid and metabolism.

Indigo Dynamic quality of being, highly energized personality, capable of projection, influencing other people, organization skills, low boredom threshold. Indigo relates to the sinuses.

Violet Abstract intuition, spiritual activity or information, trance mediumship, clairvoyance, heart or stomach trouble, theraputic healing, transmutation, arrogance, superiority, protection. Violet relates to the pineal and pituatary glands.

Recommended Reading

Edward, John. *One Last Time: A Psychic Medium Speaks to Those We Have Loved and Lost.* New York: Berkeley Publishing Group, 2004.

A good introduction to the inner world of a medium.

Hogarth, Robin. *Educating Intuition.* Chicago, Ill.: University of Chicago Press, 2001.

A helpful guide to encouraging the use of intuition, particularly valuable in educational settings.

McTaggart, Lynne. *The Field: The Quest for the Secret Force of the Universe.* New York: HarperCollins, 2002.

A fascinating read and fine introduction to a difficult topic by an investigative journalist.

Myers, David G. *Intuition: Its Powers and Perils.* New Haven, Conn.: Yale University Press, 2002.

A relentlessly skeptical view but intriguing reading nonetheless. Features 56 pages of endnotes.

Pert, Candace B. *Molecules of Emotion: Why You Feel the Way You Feel.* New York: Scribner, 1997.

"I have come to believe that science, at its very core, is a spiritual endeavor," writes Pert. (p. 315).

Reed, Henry. *Edgar Cayce on Channeling Your Higher Self: Studies in Surface Science and Catalysis.* New York: Warner Books, 1989.

A fine introduction to Cayce's works written in an approachable style. A classic.

Schwartz, G. *The Afterlife Experiments:Breakthrough Scientific Evidence of Life After Death.* New York: Pocket Books, 2002.

Recounts the experiments in mediumship that led to the HBO documentary, Life Afterlife, featuring John Edward, George Anderson and other mediums.

Sheldrake, Rupert. *The Sense of Being Stared at and Other Aspects of the Extended Mind.* New York: Crown Publishers, 2003.

Innovative book by a scientist who postulates that our minds extend beyond our brains. Well researched.

Shumsky, Susan G. *Exploring Chakras.* Franklin Lakes, N.J.: New Page Books, 2003.

A useful guide to how to work with your chakras and awaken the divine light within.

Skafte, Dianne. *When Oracles Speak: Understanding the Signs and Symbols All Around Us.* Wheaton, Ill.: Quest Books, 2000.

A historical view interweaves with the author's narrative of her own experiences and results in a fascinating read.

Tolle, Eckhart. *The Power of Now: A Guide to Spiritual Enlightenment.* Novato, Calif.: New World Library, 1999.

A modern classic written following a profound spiritually transformative experience (STE).

Van Praagh, James. *Talking to Heaven: A Medium's Message of Life After Death.* New York: Signet Books, 1999.

The first best-selling book by a modern-day medium.

Wegner, Daniel M. *The Illusion of Conscious Will.* Cambridge, Mass.: Bradford Books/The MIT Press, 2002.

Introduces the reader to a hidden world rife with aspects of ourselves that introspection may never reveal. Fascinating to read, although academic in tone.

Wicker, Chrisine. *Lily Dale: The True Story of the Town that Talks to the Dead.* San Francisco, Calif.: HarperSanFrancisco, 2003.

Lauren Thibodeau is a catalyst for Wicker's self-awareness in this intriguing, best-selling narrative.

Wills-Brandon, Carla. *A Glimpse of Heaven: The Remarkable World of Spiritually Transformative Experiences.* Avon, MA: Adams Media, 2004.

Approachable and anecdotal.

Wilson, Timothy D. *Strangers to Ourselves: Discovering the Adaptive Unconscious.* Cambridge, Mass.: The Belknap Press of Harvard University Press, 2002.

Suggests that too much introspection may muddle things even more. Approachable writing style for an academic work.

Wolf, Stacey. *Psychic Living : A Complete Guide to Enhancing Your Life.* New York: Paraview Pocket Books, 2004.

A witty take on practical applications of psychic development. Ideal for younger readers and those new to the world of intuition.

WEB RESOURCES

The following are resources you may find helpful as you develop a deeper level of intuitive inner wisdom.

Mediumship and Intuition Development

SeekersCircle.com
Online intuitive development, operated by the author. Free practice message boards, free healing requests, chats with experts and many other resources. An active international online community.

VanPraagh.com
One of the most active Websites about mediumship, maintained by author and medium James Van Praagh. The author is listed among the recommended mediums.

JohnEdward.net
The first medium to host his own television show, John Edward has expanded awareness about mediumship. The author wrote for his Website by request and is among the mediums his office recommends.

ForeverFamilyFoundation.org
Affiliated with mediumship researcher Gary E. Schwarz, Ph.D., this group tests and certifies mediums.

Parapsychology and Research

Institute of Noetic Sciences
Ions.org conducts and sponsors leading-edge research into the potentials and powers of consciousness—including percpetions, beliefs, attention,

intention, and intuition—while maintaining a commitment to scientific rigor.

Laboratory for Advances in Consciousness and Health (lach.web.arizona.edu)

Founded in 2006, affiliated with University of Arizona researcher and author Gary E. Schwartz, Ph.D., it researches consciousness in eight areas, including groups, animals, and event "ETs."

Exceptional Human Experience Network (Ehe.org)

An educational, research, adn informtion resource organization studying all types of anomalous (out of the ordinary) experiences.

TASTE   (issc-taste.org/main/introduction/shtml)

TASTE is an online journal devoted to trascendent experiences that scientists have reported, and allows scientists to express these experiences in a psychologically (and professionally) safe place.

Parapsychological Association (parapsych.org)

An international professional organization of scientists and scholars engaged in the study of "psi" (or "psychic") experiences, such as telepathy, clairvoyance, psychokinesis, psychic healing, and precognition.

General Spirituality

belief.net

Information about many paths to self understanding, from martial arts to sacred texts and traditional religions. A comprehensive resource.

Grief and Bereavement Support

compassionatefriends.org

A national self-help organization offering friendship and understanding to bereaved parents, grandparents, and sibling. Features an extensive resource list to help locate the exact grief support you need, frompet loss to "twinless twins" to aircraft casualty loss. Local chapters and conferences.

griefnet.org

Offers online support through numbereous e-mail support groups with specialties including grief-pet, grief-violence, grief-suicide, and horrific-loss.

INDEX

ABOUT THE AUTHOR

Lauren Thibodeau holds a Ph.D. in counseling as well as two masters degrees, an M.Ed. and an M.B.A. She is a graduate faculty member of Atlantic University.

A nationally certified counselor and a professional member of the National Speakers Association, "Dr. Lauren" works with individuals and organizations in helping them access and apply their intuitive intelligence. She has consulted with and taught thousands of people to better employ their Knowing, including police detectives, professionals, corporate executives, entertainers, and entrepreneurs. Dr. Thibodeau was in corporate management before launching her intuitive consulting practice.

Veteran of hundreds of media appearances, Dr. Thibodeau has appeared in several programs broadcast on television in the United States, Canada, and the U.K. Dr. Thibodeau also is the chief visionary behind SeekersCircle.com, the top-ranking site for intuition development and self-growth through inner wisdom, which features an active online community of thousands.

Based in New York City, she presents internationally at conferences and workshops. Learn more about her work at her Website, *www.DrLauren.com.*

Made in the USA
Lexington, KY
14 March 2012